1066

1066

A Guide to the Battles and the Campaigns

Michael Livingston and
Kelly DeVries

Pen & Sword
MILITARY

First published in Great Britain in 2020 by
Pen & Sword Military
An imprint of
Pen & Sword Books Ltd
Yorkshire – Philadelphia

ISBN 978 1 52675 197 3

Typeset by Mac Style
Printed and bound in India by
Replika Press Pvt. Ltd.

Pen & Sword Books Limited incorporates the imprints of Atlas,
Archaeology, Aviation, Discovery, Family History, Fiction,
History, Maritime, Military, Military Classics, Politics, Select,
Transport, True Crime, Air World, Frontline Publishing, Leo
Cooper, Remember When, Seaforth Publishing, The Praetorian
Press, Wharncliffe Local History, Wharncliffe Transport,
Wharncliffe True Crime
and White Owl.

For a complete list of Pen & Sword titles please contact

PEN & SWORD BOOKS LIMITED
47 Church Street, Barnsley, South Yorkshire, S70 2AS, England
E-mail: enquiries@pen-and-sword.co.uk
Website: www.pen-and-sword.co.uk

Or

PEN AND SWORD BOOKS
1950 Lawrence Rd, Havertown, PA 19083, USA
E-mail: Uspen-and-sword@casematepublishers.com
Website: www.penandswordbooks.com

CONTENTS

Acknowledgements   vi
Introduction   1

Chapter 1   The Old Kingdom   5

Chapter 2   William and Normandy   22
                  Tour One: Origins of the Conqueror   41

Chapter 3   The Norwegian Invasion   59
                  Tour Two: Tostig's Journey   78

Chapter 4   William's Road to Hastings   101
                  Tour Three: Pevensey Castle and Surrounds   108

Chapter 5   The Battle of Hastings   124
                  Tour Four: Battle Abbey and Surrounds   150

Chapter 6   William's March to London   168
                  Tour Five: William's March   183

Further Reading   204
Index   207

ACKNOWLEDGEMENTS

We owe thanks to a great many friends, family and colleagues whose support enabled us to complete this book. Among these, specific nods of gratitude go to Peter Konieczny, the extraordinary editor of *Medieval Warfare Magazine*, who first suggested that we write on the invasion of England for a 2017 special issue – articles that prompted Rupert Harding to ask us to write this guidebook. We also owe thanks to Stephen Chumbley for so ably shepherding this project from manuscript to completed book. Last but hardly least, Robert Woosnam-Savage and Samuel Livingston cannot be thanked enough, not just for their exceptional insights and good-natured patience during research visits to those sites discussed in these pages, but also for their welcome reminder that history is meant to be shared.

Michael and Kelly
Charleston, SC
April 2020

INTRODUCTION

At the end of that October day – after the sun had set, after the last of the fleeing men had been run down – the victors joined the beasts and carrion-fowl making their claims on the valuable dead. Dark shadows moved against roving flickers of torchlight. Whispered voices joined the scattered moans of the dying on the

In this 1875 sculpture, Charles Augustus William Wilke imagines Edith Swan-neck finding Harold's body after the battle. The sculpture sits, exposed to the elements, in the West Marina Gardens in Hastings (A259 and Sea Road).

crisp air, echoing across the hillsides. Corpses were turned over. The leather lashings of armours were hurriedly slashed, buckles and rivets scattering away to be trampled into the blood-wet earth.

Mourners came, picking their way through the dark to identify friends and loved ones. And the monks came too, accompanied by the rumbling carts that would carry the dead to blessed ground and an eternal rest, praying both for those on the field and those at home who wouldn't learn of their losses until their sons, fathers and husbands never returned.

Among the wives, mothers, lovers and children who wept in the days after the battle was Edith – Ealdgyth in the English tongue – the common-law wife or mistress of the man who had been king. Only a few months earlier, Harold Godwinson had married another Edith, the daughter of the earl of Mercia, but history has deemed this second, potentially bigamous marriage to be one of political convenience to the Crown. His heart, it is thought, was forever bound to the first Edith, who came to the battlefield to find his body.

William, the man who'd caused the death of her husband, was a bastard son who had risen to be duke of Normandy when he landed on the shores of England. His beachhead was at Hastings, not far down the road from the field of carnage that Edith searched, and the battle, in time, would take that name: the Battle of Hastings. Now both duke of Normandy and king of England, William the Bastard, by right of this day and the days to come, would forever be known by a new cognomen: William the Conqueror.

Death in the melee of a medieval battle was never clean. Wounds were open. Viscera were everywhere. Blood and tissue streaked everything.

Harold's body had been even further torn apart. The men who'd struck him down took vengeance for fallen friends of their own. So badly was he mutilated that Edith alone was able to identify his body, recognizing it by certain marks that she knew.

At least, that's one story, from the hand of the unknown author of the chronicle of Waltham Abbey, which Harold had founded – and to which, according to this account, his remains were afterward taken for burial.

Another story – this one from the hand of William of Poitiers, c.1071 – has it that Edith made no such identification. William's men had already identified the body and it was Harold's mother, Gytha, who asked for it. It's unlikely that she was able to be there in person. Word of what had happened at the Battle of Hastings would have travelled quickly, spread from rider to more riders across the dark countryside of England. Thus would it have come to Harold's mother, who sent her own message flying back to William: her son's weight in gold in exchange for the body.

William refused. Instead he gave the body to a man named William Malet, who was ordered to find a place to bury it, quietly and secretly. The Conqueror, it seems, was uninterested in having the grave of Harold serve as a symbolic focus for any resistance to his new rule. Exactly where Malet took the body is unknown – he did his job well – but another early source, the anonymous *Carmen de Hastingae Proelio*, written before 1068, suggests that he took it down the road that the Normans had already secured: the road back south, toward Hastings and the sea. There, if *this* story is to be believed, he found a suitable spot atop the cliffs and unceremoniously buried the man with an epitaph written on stone:

By the duke's commands, O Harold, you rest here a king,
That you may still be guardian of the shore and sea.

It might be tempting to see something romantic in the image of the last Anglo-Saxon king resting upon the Saxon Shore, but it is unlikely that William intended such a thing. His impulse was not romance, but mockery: the centuries-old Saxon Shore defences had fallen. More than that, wherever Malet had taken him, Harold's grave was set upon no hallowed ground. William had defeated him in this world and such was his confidence in the righteousness of his own cause – and the wickedness of Harold's – that he hoped the horror of Hastings would follow Harold into the next world.

In the coming years, his throne finally secured, William would order an abbey built on the battlefield both to give thanks for his victory and to give penance by praying for the souls of those who perished in making it so. The high altar of the abbey's chapel, it was ordered, would be built on the spot where Harold's body was supposedly found upon the battlefield. Though Battle Abbey lies in

The stone marking the site of Battle Abbey's high altar today. (*Michael Livingston*)

ruins, the place of the altar remains marked there today, a pale stone block amid quiet green grasses.

This book is a guide to the events leading up to that marker: the historical crossroads of Harold's death and William's victory as it unfolded more than 950 years ago. It is a guide to the present ground, following in the footsteps of Harold's and William's campaigns from the sources available to us – including that portion of the Norman Conquest that is so carefully sewn into one of the most famous artefacts of the Middle Ages: the Bayeux Tapestry. It is the story of two great men, who in coming together in this place, in this battle, would change the history of England.

And with England, the world.

Chapter 1

THE OLD KINGDOM

So strongly does the Battle of Hastings loom in English history that it can be easy to think of the English crown that William wrested from Harold as an ancient thing. In truth, though, the Anglo-Saxons were relative newcomers to the island that would come to be named for the Angles among them. They came in a series of waves from the areas around lowland Germany in the fifth and sixth centuries AD: bands of Angles, Saxons, Myrgings, Jutes and others. Before them, the island had been held by the Romans, who called it Britannia: a name reflecting the Britons, the people who had been there before them.

It took time for the English to push back against the peoples on the island, yet even as they began to stabilize their claims on the land with a handful of loosely affiliated kingdoms that still mark the English landscape today – Wessex (kingdom of the West Saxons), Essex (the East Saxons), East Anglia (the East Angles) and so forth – the various tribes that would become the English found themselves facing another threat rising from the sea in their wake: Scandinavian raiders, popularly known as Vikings, arrived on the island's shores with a violent attack on the rich monastery of Lindisfarne in 793. Not long afterward, raiders became invaders: migratory waves from Scandinavia that flooded and conquered kingdom after kingdom, until in 878 King Alfred (r. 886–99) managed to stop them at the Battle of Ethandun. Still, after Alfred's death, the Norse and the English pushed and pulled at each other across the landscape and more than once it was a Scandinavian who sat upon the throne of a place increasingly called England.

It was only in 937 that a king was able to claim a crown that in some measure matches our image of England. In that year, the grandson of Alfred the Great gathered an enormous army and fought a fierce battle against a combined force of Scots, Strathclyde Britons and Irish

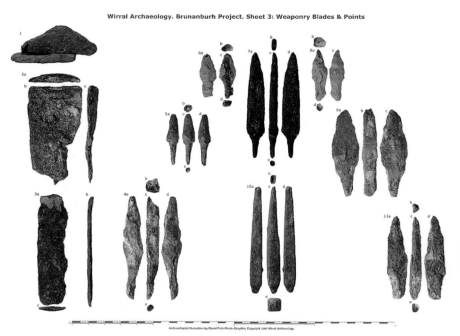

Wirral Archaeology. Brunanburh Project. Sheet 3: Weaponry Blades & Points

In recent years, archaeologists have uncovered a staggering number of artefacts from the presumed site of the Battle of Brunanburh. No such artefacts have been found on the traditional site of Hastings. (*Michael Livingston*)

Vikings who had set their differences aside in order to construct an army with the single purpose of driving the hated English back to the sea. But at Brunanburh – a place once as lost to us as Harold's grave – King Athelstan (r. 924–39) beat them. Coins minted during his reign read 'King of all Britain'. So famous was this moment that for generations afterward the Battle of Brunanburh would be called 'the Great Battle'.

Until Hastings, that is.

The cause of Hastings – a battle so impactful that its shadow effectively smothered Brunanburh in popular memory – was very different in character. Whereas Brunanburh had been a battle of existential survival for the English kingdom, Hastings would be a battle of political vengeance that would end it.

A Dozen Kings of England

Athelstan's victory at Brunanburh in 937 had firmly established a kingdom, but it hardly did the same for his dynasty. True, his two brothers, Edmund I (r. 939–46) and Eadred (r. 946–55), had carried on his immediate legacy, followed by Edmund's sons Eadwig (r. 955–9) and Edgar (r. 959–75). But the throne was then contested among Edgar's sons: his eldest, Edward the Martyr, was crowned and ruled until his murder in 978, after which the other contesting son, Athelred (r. 1014–16), took the throne. He would come to be known as the Unready, a name that meant in its time 'ill-advised', though in retrospect 'unready' could fit just as well.

What Athelred wasn't ready for was the resurgence of Danish hostilities beginning in the 980s. Disaster at the Battle of Maldon in 991, in which a raiding Danish force annihilated the local English militia at the royal mint-town of Maldon, prompted Athelred to begin paying the king of the Danes a tribute, the Danegeld, to keep English shores safe. But peace would not hold on either side and in 1013 King Sweyn Forkbeard of Denmark successfully invaded the island. Exiled, Athelred fled across the English Channel to Normandy: his wife, Emma, was the daughter of the duke of Normandy and they found support and safety there.

King Sweyn died in 1014 and Athelred managed to return from his exile to rule for two more years, but they were anything but peaceful. First he had to fight Sweyn's son, Cnut, and then his own, Edmund Ironside. Cnut, initially made to flee the island, came back in force in 1016 and took the crown. Athelred died just a few months later and Edmund Ironside died that November. As a result, the new king of England was once again a Dane: Cnut the Great would rule as king of England – and later king of both Denmark and Norway as well.

Importantly for what was to come, Cnut married Athelred's widow, Emma of Normandy. While this marriage was in large measure intended to make peace between the English and Danes in England, it also had the effect of saving the lives of Athelred's children by Emma: Alfred and Edward, who were being raised in the court of Normandy.

Cnut's long reign saw the rise of a man who would loom large in the history of the next decades: Godwin, the powerful earl of Wessex. Just four years into Cnut's reign, Godwin had risen from relative

The Kings of England to 1066

Alfred the Great	c.886–99	Wessex
Edward the Elder	899–924	Wessex
Athelstan	924–39	Wessex
Edmund I	939–46	Wessex
Eadred	946–55	Wessex
Eadwig	955–9	Wessex
Edgar	959–75	Wessex
Edward the Martyr	975–8	Wessex
Athelred the Unready	978–1013	Wessex
Sweyn Forkbeard	1013–14	Denmark
Athelred the Unready	1014–16	Wessex
Edmund II Ironside	1016	Wessex
Cnut the Great	1016–35	Denmark
Harald I Harefoot	1035–40	Denmark
Harthacnut	1040–2	Denmark
Edward the Confessor	1042–66	Wessex
Harold II Godwinson	1066	Godwin
Edgar Atheling	1066	Wessex
William I the Conqueror	1066–87	Normandy

obscurity to hold the rich earldom of Wessex and he would become one of the foremost power brokers of his age. After the death of Cnut in 1035, Godwin threw his support behind the expected heir to the tribes of the Danes and English, Cnut's son by Emma, Harthacnut.

However, Harthacnut's need to defend his Scandinavian holdings prevented him from coming to claim the crown of England. In his absence, another one of Cnut's sons (not by Emma), Harold Harefoot, served as England's regent before being crowned himself in 1037. Godwin had initially stood in opposition to Harold's coronation, but he appears to have been a man of political flexibility. When Athelred and Emma's son, Alfred, arrived on English shores in 1036, Earl Godwin handed him over to Harold's forces. Alfred was blinded and died.

Harold Harefoot himself died in 1040, at which time Harthacnut indeed claimed the throne. He brought Godwin to trial over his half-brother Alfred's death. Though it might seem that Godwin's star was diminished, the death of Harthacnut in 1042 brought him and his family to greater positions than ever. With the support of Godwin, the crown now passed to the last of Emma's children by Athelred: the dead Alfred's brother, Edward. History would come to know him as Edward the Confessor and he had spent almost the entirety of the last two decades of his life in the court of the duke of Normandy. Three years after Edward's coronation, he was married to Edith, the daughter of Earl Godwin – the man who, despite his lack of a crown, might well have been the most powerful man in England.

In the century following the Battle of Brunanburh, then, almost a dozen men from at least four modern nationalities had sat upon the throne of England. This volatility well reflects the measure of what it meant to be a king: a man needed bloodlines, but he also needed to back up his own blood with the blood of others. A good king, as the opening of the great Old English poem *Beowulf* observes around the year 1000, was a man with both a rightful claim to the throne and the strength to back it up:

> Beaw was well-known, his name spread wide:
> King Scyld's heir in Scandinavian lands.
> Thus should a youth give rise to good
> through treasured favours in his father's house,
> so that in future years willing friends
> will stand beside him when war comes,
> and the people uphold him – with praised deeds
> will one prosper among the people! (*Beowulf*, lines 18–25)

The Crisis for the Crown

King Edward the Confessor, from the Bayeux Tapestry. (*Musée de la Tapisserie de Bayeux*)

Given the political chaos that England had seen prior to Edward the Confessor's rule, the matter of succession was inevitably going to be a source of concern as the years passed. But it was especially so since this king – whether by choice, condition or just dumb luck – produced no heir through his marriage to Edith.

Questions of succession seem to have grown louder when, in 1051, the relationship between the king and the powerful family of his wife went sour. An initial strain was Edward's refusal to recognize the election of a member of Godwin's family as Archbishop of Canterbury; Edward instead pushed through the election of a Norman, Robert of Jumièges. Not long afterward, matters came to a head when the earl refused Edward's order to punish the people of Dover after they rioted against the visiting Count Eustace II of Boulogne, a close ally of the king. Though they were his wife's family, Edward banished the earl and all his heirs. Godwin himself, along with his wife Gytha and his sons Sweyn, Tostig and Gyrth, fled to Flanders. His sons Harold and Leofwine took refuge in Ireland. King Edward placed his wife, Godwin's daughter, in a convent.

A year later, though, the family returned and the public rallied in their support. Edward found himself with few options beyond restoring their lands and titles. He granted as much, though it could not have been with a great deal of pleasure.

Trusting Evidence

One of the obvious problems in sorting out the events surrounding Hastings is the fact that so many potential sources of information have disappeared over the course of almost 1,000 years. Less obvious, but no less impactful, we face the problem that the sources that did survive are deeply biased. William and his successors went to great efforts to paper over his conquest in the most literal fashion possible: by writing their own versions of what had happened and eliminating competing stories, they shaped history to their liking. At almost every turn, then, we have to question whether informants like William of Poitiers – who was William the Conqueror's chaplain! – are telling us the truth about what happened … or only what they want us to *think* had happened.

Though we have no record of it, some historians believe that this whole affair in 1051–2 prompted the childless Edward to take steps to promise the crown of England to William, the duke of Normandy. Certainly this is the kind of situation that Norman propagandists wanted to suggest during and after William's conquest. Other historians, however, point out that even if Edward felt he had the authority to make such a promise, he almost certainly would have done so in a measurably public way that would have left verifiable traces. Keeping any such arrangements hush-hush would surely defeat the purpose of confirming an heir entirely.

That there were connections between William and Edward cannot be doubted, however. The two men were cousins – Edward's grandfather, Richard I of Normandy, was William's great-grandfather – but more essential to any rationale for a promise would have been Normandy's important role in the history of the English crown through this period. Emma was from there, Edward had been raised there and Norman influence had been strong in bringing him the crown. William's career was also in the ascendant. His illegitimate

William, the duke of Normandy, from the Bayeux Tapestry. (*Musée de la Tapisserie de Bayeux*)

birth had initially brought several rivals into rebellion, but with the help of King Henry I of France he had crushed them at Val-ès-Dunes in 1047. Then, in 1049, a marriage was arranged between William and Matilda, the daughter of Count Baldwin V of Flanders. Though papal objections would prevent the match from being made for several years, William was in an undoubtedly influential position for the marriage arrangement to have been made at all, as we will detail in the next chapter.

Sweyn Godwinson

Godwin's eldest son, Sweyn, three times had to seek safety in the court of Flanders: first, in 1046–7, because he was charged with kidnapping the abbess of Leominster and force her into a marriage; second, in 1049–50, because he had directly caused the murder of the very cousin who helped negotiate his return from the first exile; and third, in 1051 when the entire Godwin family was exiled. For his (many) sins, Sweyn determined to walk barefoot to Jerusalem. He died on his return, according to our sources, his penance fulfilled.

Godwin himself would die in 1053, leaving his eldest remaining son Harold in charge of his estates. Over the next decade and more, the children of Godwin grew more and more powerful within the kingdom. Harold took his father's place as the earl of Wessex. Tostig became the earl of Northumbria. Gyrth became the earl of East Anglia.

Harold I Godwinson, from the Bayeux Tapestry. (*Musée de la Tapisserie de Bayeux*)

And Leofwine became earl of Kent. Even more, Harold became close to the king in a way his father never was. For much of the rest of Edward the Confessor's reign, Harold served as not just his loyal and able right-hand man, but in many cases his de facto replacement in governance: Harold's name in this period is ascribed on documents beside titles such as '*sub-regulus*' (under-king) or '*dux Anglorum*' (leader of the English). It must have been plain to see that Harold Godwinson, by virtue of both his position and being the head of his powerful family, would be able to make a claim for the throne himself.

In 1063 Harold and his younger brother Tostig jointly led the king's forces on a successful invasion of Gruffydd ap Llywelyn's kingdom of Gwynedd in northern Wales: Harold led a fleet attacking from Bristol in the south while Tostig led an army overland from Northumbria. They met at Gruffydd's capital of Rhuddlan, only to find that the king had fled into Snowdonia, where he was killed by his own men. It was a remarkably effective campaign – so much so that almost a century later John of Salisbury would praise it in his guide to political rule, the *Policraticus*.

Attacking Wales

At the very end of the twelfth century, Gerald of Wales reports that he had encountered numerous inscribed stones saying 'Harold Was The Victor Here' celebrating the victory of Harold and Tostig Godwinson over Gruffydd ap Llywelyn. None of these inscribed stones remain today, nor does Gruffydd's Rhuddlan exist any longer, although archaeologists have located its remains. When Edward I built his massive castle on a hill overlooking the village in 1282, he also diverted the river away from the Welsh village, forcing the villagers to move nearer to the castle.

Despite his high title, Tostig's position in Northumbria was far less important and quite distant from the royal court in London – although as a favourite of his sister, Edith, Edward's queen, he does seem to have spent a lot of time there rather than in York. Had he spent more time in Northumbria, the earl might have developed better relations with the local nobles. It wasn't long before Tostig's subjects began accusing him of levying heavy taxes (using the money for his own goods and endowments) and, worse, that he was behind the assassination of three of their northern leaders: Gamal, Ulf and Gospatric.

Kirkdale Sundial

A surviving witness to Tostig as earl of Northumbria is a canonical sundial mounted above the church doors of St. Gregory's Minster in Kirkdale, North Yorkshire, commemorating the rebuilding of the church c.1055. The inscription on the sundial is in Old English:

> Orm Gamal suna bohte Sanctus Gregorius Minster ðonne hit wæs æl tobrocan and tofalan and he hit let macan newan from grunde Christe and Sanctus Gregorius in Eadward dagum cyning and in Tosti dagum eorl.

In Modern English:

> Orm, son of Gamal, bought St Gregory's Minster when it was all broken and fallen and he had it made anew from the ground up for Christ and St Gregory in the days of Edward the king and Tostig the earl.

It is possible that the Gamal mentioned in the inscription is the same Gamal whom the Northumbrian rebels accused Tostig of killing in 1065. In addition to the fact that its inscription is important for naming the earl and Orm, the Kirkdale Sundial is often noted for possibly revealing how much English had come to dominate the linguistic landscape of a region that had been settled by Vikings.

Drawing of the Kirkdale Sundial showing the inscription which mentions the church's reconstruction during the earlship of Tostig Godwinson.

So it was that in October 1065, following the death of the last of these men, Gospatric, an armed delegation approached King Edward looking for justice, accusing not just Tostig of the murder, but also, shockingly, Queen Edith. At Northampton, where they stopped to meet with the king, who was then convalescing at his palace in Oxford, they were joined by Edwin, the earl of Mercia, whose brother, Morkere, they wanted to be earl. Harold was sent by Edward to sort the whole thing out.

Up to this time, Harold and Tostig seem to have been friendly and supportive of one another. Harold offered concessions to the rebels and he threatened military suppression. But the Northumbrians would not back down. Harold quickly realized that there was no way for Tostig to continue as earl. Although Tostig had become a

More than a Sibling Rivalry?

Evidently the tale of two brothers simply falling out was insufficiently dramatic for later medieval English historians. Already by the second quarter of the twelfth century the story was changing. In his *Historia Anglorum* (*English History*), Henry of Huntingdon claims that in 1064 at the royal court in Windsor, a drunken Tostig was thrown to the ground by his brother after pulling his hair. Humiliated, Tostig travelled to Harald's manor in Hereford where the earl of Essex was preparing a banquet for the king. There he dismembered his brother's servants, adding their body parts to the wine, which he tried to serve the king. Edward, already considered a saint when Henry was writing – although he would not be officially canonized until 1161 – knew that the wine was fouled and demanded that Tostig be outlawed.

Half a century later, a Cistercian monk, Aelred of Rielvaux, wrote a different version of the rivalry, changing both the date – to their childhood – and place – to their father's house. There Edward observed a vicious fight between the two boys, tossed off as child's play by Godwin. Not so, said the king, but a portent of problems ahead, '… in the end the stronger will outlaw the weaker and over-throw his rebelling brother. Yet it will be only a short time before the death of the first is avenged by the destruction of the second.'

favourite of the king, Edward had no choice but to agree. Within a month Tostig was stripped of his title and banished, exiled from the court and England. Tostig was furious, accused Harold of plotting against him, then fled with his family to the court of Flanders, where his brother-in-law, Baldwin V, was count.

At Christmas time, only a month or so after Tostig was banished, the *witena-gemot* – the most powerful and connected men of the realm, traditionally charged with naming and advising the king – gathered at Westminster.

It's hard for the observer today, looking across the landscape of Westminster's modern concrete buildings, to imagine what it would have been like at the time. Much of what we now see as a district of London was then an island beside the Thames, bordered by the river and the tributaries of the Tyburn. Those banks, mapped roughly today, would run under 10 Downing Street, along the length of the lake in St. James's Park, then south and west along Buckingham Palace Road, before cutting back to the Thames via Grosvenor Canal. It was called Thorney (Thorn Island), so named for its harsh vegetation, and in centuries past it had been little more than a marshy isle that functioned as part of a tidal ford across the Thames: until the construction of London Bridge, it may have been the easternmost crossing point of that wide river. For this reason, the Romans had paved the road to either side of the ford, creating what would become known as Watling Street, which would ultimately run from Canterbury to Wroxeter. Today, aside from the few water features that mark its former shores, the memory of the island survives only in Thorney Street, a short stretch of road behind MI5 headquarters at the end of Victoria Tower Gardens.

Despite such inhospitable ground, a church is said to have been built on Thorney in the seventh century by Mellitus, an early missionary and the first bishop of London. King Edgar then established a Benedictine monastery there and beginning in the 1040s Edward the Confessor began construction on expanding the site with a massive complex: a Norman-styled stone abbey and an adjacent royal palace. Little of this construction still remains above ground. The present Westminster Abbey, built in the Gothic style, replaced Edward's in the thirteenth century: its Pyx Chamber and undercroft are the only remains of Edward's abbey visible today. Edward's palace is gone, too, its traces erased by demolition and multiple fires. The oldest building still on the site is Westminster Hall, which was built by King William II; the present Houses of Parliament date to the end of the nineteenth century.

That the *witena-gemot* should have gathered that Christmas is hardly unusual. It was typical for them to meet at mid-winter. Yet this year was to have an added solemnity in that Edward's abbey – a structure that he likely considered the crowning achievement of his reign – was going to be consecrated. It was indeed an extraordinary structure and people might already have begun to call the place 'West Minster', marking it as a counter-point to St. Paul's in London, the minster two miles to the north-east.

But what ought to have been a joyous time was sombre and full of concern. In November, just after the banishment of Tostig, Edward had fallen ill, perhaps suffering a minor stroke. He recovered, but then on Christmas Eve he was struck down again. When his magnificent

The Pyx Chamber beneath Westminster Abbey.

church was consecrated on Childermas, 28 December, the king was not present, though he would have heard the peal of its bells from his bed in the new palace next door. As the new year of 1066 dawned, it was clear that the childless king, who was moving between delirium and coma, was dying. The issue of succession was no longer one of theoretical claims. The crown would go to someone.

In theory, the *witena-gemot* could choose anyone they thought fit and the twisting road that the crown had taken since Brunanburh meant there was no shortage of men who could have pressed for the throne. Edmund Ironside's son, Edward, might have been a logical successor, but he had died in 1057. That left his potential claim to Edgar Atheling, a boy of 13. But despite having been raised within Edward's own household since the death of his father, there is little indication that he was given much consideration for the task of taking over the crown. Across the North Sea, King Sweyn II Estridsson could theoretically have had a claim, too, as both the king of Denmark and a grandson of Sweyn Forkbeard. His neighbour to the north, King Harald Hardrada of Norway, could also make a claim. In either case, there is no evidence that they were ever put forward.

Oath-breaking

William of Normandy and his supporters claimed that in taking the throne Harold Godwinson had broken his word to him. Hariulf, a monk writing across the English Channel in the monastery of St-Riquier, likewise saw Harold as an oath-breaker, but not to William. Instead, the monk writes, Harold wrongly broke his promise to Edward that he would support the king's cousin, Alfgar. There was an Alfgar, who as earl of Mercia was a rival to the Godwin family but whose daughter, Edith, would marry Harold Godwinson a short time before his death at Hastings. Yet Alfgar died before Hastings and he wasn't a cousin to Edward. Is it possible that Hariulf meant Edgar Atheling? If so, might there have been a promise made to the boy as well?

The king's opinion would have held much sway, yet it doesn't appear that he had ever formally announced his intentions. Had he already promised the throne to William of Normandy? If so, had he changed his mind in the years since? And what of Harold, who had been effectively ruling the kingdom for some ten years?

According to the *Vita Edwardi Regis*, which was written shortly after the event, the king awoke on 4 January and appeared to be lucid. His wife, Edith, was there, as were both Harold and the Archbishop of Canterbury. Also there was Robert FitzWimark, a half-Norman friend of Edward's, whose presence is important to note: when it came to what happened next, William of Normandy and his allies had every interest in telling an alternate tale to the one that would soon circulate. They did not. Everyone, it seems, heard the same thing.

Edward told them of a dream he had of his kingdom beset with war and destruction for a year and a day. Then he gave his love to his queen, praying for her and thanking her for being beside him 'like a loving daughter'. Next, before them all, he gave Edith into the protection of Harold, her brother – and with her, the protection of the kingdom. More words were exchanged. He explained how he wished to be buried. Then Edward the Confessor slipped back into unconsciousness. During the night, he died.

Edward the Confessor on his deathbed, from the Bayeux Tapestry. (*Musée de la Tapisserie de Bayeux*)

Amid the prayers of mourning for Edward's death and the preparations for his entombment in his newly-constructed abbey, the *witena-gemot* gathered. If they thought about the full range of the many possible claimants, they surely hoped that some of them would stand down from their claims. But if the preceding century had taught them anything, it would have been to expect that not all of them would. It might well be that they knew the act of choosing – no matter who they picked – would set them upon a path to war. They needed a proven leader, a powerful man who could unite any defence that needed to be undertaken.

Perhaps this fact, added to Edward's deathbed speech, is why they chose, on the day after Edward's death, to crown Harold Godwinson as king of England. Of all the men who could wear the crown, he was the one most ready to defend it.

And defend it he would.

The Shrine of Edward the Confessor in Westminster Abbey.

Chapter 2

WILLIAM AND NORMANDY

Sometime between the middle of 1027 and the middle of 1028, the child who would become the Conqueror was born at Falaise Castle in central Normandy. His unmarried parents, Robert and Herleva, named him William.

If it was before 6 August 1027, Robert was the brother of the duke of Normandy, who had only come to the title after the death of their father a year earlier. If it was after that date, then Robert was duke himself, after his brother's own untimely death.

Why Robert and Herleva were unmarried is a mystery, especially as it seems they had been together for quite a while by the time of William's birth. The answer most often given is that she was a commoner, the daughter of a tanner or an embalmer, and not therefore of a status to marry a duke of Normandy. But this may not be the case. Her father, Fulbert of Falaise, served as ducal chamberlain and when Herleva did marry, in 1031, it was to Herluin de Conteville, a lesser Norman noble, with whom she would bear William's two half-brothers, Odo, bishop of Bayeux, and Robert, count of Mortain, who would both accompany William on his conquest of England in 1066. It is doubtful that her marriage to Herluin would have happened if she had been a commoner.

It may have been that Robert simply did not want to marry. He was a pious man and he died – still unwed, still without legitimate issue – at Antioch on his return from a pilgrimage to Jerusalem. He was only 34, but had he followed tradition in fulfilling one of the most important duties of an upper nobleman, prince or king, he would have already been married and had a bevy of legitimate children.

As it was, that never happened. The young boy who was born that day in Falaise to Robert and Herleva was a bastard. And William would carry that label – *bastardus* in Latin chronicles and documents and *batarde* in French ones – for the rest of his life.

Concubines and Bastards

A modern Christian would condemn concubinage, but not hold an individual's bastardy against them. An eleventh-century Christian saw things in reverse: medieval noblemen were not blamed when taking on extra sexual partners, but the children born from these unions were not well treated. In defence of concubinage, Old Testament examples like David and Solomon were often held forth, although it should be noted that the same did not hold true for extra marriages: concubinage was okay; polygamy was not.

Bastard children who were recognized by their father – which was certainly not all of them – were brought into his court to be raised, often next to legitimate issue. But even fathers who recognized their bastard children did not often legitimize them and, without legitimization, they were never accorded inheritance or other privileges. They were well cared for, though, and were usually well educated, which meant that bastards often became members of the clergy, frequently in positions of authority. Those children who didn't join the clergy could marry, but while the connections to their fathers were still influential in making matches, these marriages were rarely as important as those that were arranged for legitimate children. As a result, bastard children were sometimes wed to other bastard children of noblemen.

Despite this being no fault of bastard children, the stain of illegitimacy would continue into the modern age – in the eighteenth century bastards were signed into Frederick the Great of Prussia's recruitment registers upside down to distinguish them from legitimately-born soldiers, for example. Concubinage has been discontinued, too, at least not by legal definition; although, of course, early modern and modern kings and state leaders have hardly discontinued extra-marital affairs.

Interestingly, medieval noblewomen did not have any 'bastards'. All their children were considered legitimate issues of their noble fathers – despite sometimes not looking like them!

William was legitimized by his father, Robert, duke of Normandy, though when this took place isn't easy to determine. Robert may have legitimized William at birth, if he had no plans to marry. Later legend, propagated by the late-twelfth-century writer Wace, has Herleva on the morning after William's conception prophesying that she had in her womb a tree that would cover all of Normandy in its shadow – which no doubt would have influenced Robert's legitimization of his bastard son if it were true!

Adelaide of Normandy

The legitimization of William's half-sister, Adelaide of Normandy, who was born to yet another of Robert's concubines, allowed her to be married to three high-ranking noblemen: Enguerrand II, count of Ponthieu (this marriage would be annulled in 1049 on grounds of consanguinity), Lambert II, count of Lens, who was killed in battle in 1054 and Odo, count of Champagne.

William's illegitimate birth had no bearing on his ascension to the ducal throne at the death of his father, but his age did: he was only 7 or 8 years old. Ultimately, he may not have survived as duke had he not the support of his uncle, Robert, the very powerful Archbishop of Rouen, and Henry I, the king of France. Yet even their influence could not stave off disruptions and rebellions: during the first decade and more of his becoming duke, his minority status would be abused and fought over. One powerful noble after another sought to control him, some even retaining him in their custody – essentially imprisoning him. In some ways this was simply the 'normality' of the time: nobles throughout Europe frequently feuded over territorial and political power. Strong lords survived, even prospered; weak ones did neither. Those with powerful supporters often relied on their protection to get through the more difficult periods. As a young duke, no matter what strength he displayed early on, he was a target of many who wished to enrich their positions and holdings at his expense. This left the duchy of Normandy weak and disunited. At one point, in 1046, the forces against him grew so powerful that William fled to the court of Henry I, until his supporters were able to beat back some of the threats.

Ironically, it was this time away from his duchy that afforded William his first military experience. Throughout his youth, advisors and teachers would have schooled him in riding horses and fighting with arms and in armour: his contemporaries frequently comment on William's size and strength. He might even have been taught strategy and tactics. But before the Battle of Val-ès-Dunes in 1047, he had not experienced combat.

During the months of his self-imposed exile, William's would-be usurpers, Guy de Brionne (his cousin), Nigel, viscount of the Cotentin, and Ranulf, viscount of the Bessin, had been gathering their forces, which some sources ultimately numbered at 25,000. This is no doubt an exaggeration, although it's likely symbolic of the extensive opposition to William's rule at the time. Against them stood William's supporters with aid from the French army – numbering around 10,000, a more credible figure.

Unfortunately, no contemporary record details what happened during the battle. Wace does so, but he was writing at the end of the twelfth century and he is known more for his embellishments than his accuracies. What he writes is simple, though, and similar in many ways to what medieval battles were like – unlike Hastings, as we will see, which by all accounts was unusual as to its length and constant action. Wace says that Henry and William marched into Normandy and met up with those allied against William at an unidentified place 12.5 miles (20km) south-east of Caen known as Val-ès-Dunes. Initially, the king and duke took up a defensive position, possibly because they were outnumbered. But after withstanding what the king and duke deemed was a less than impressive charge, they counter-attacked, quickly sending the usurpers' forces into rout. Several of those in flight drowned trying to cross the Orne River in an attempt to gain the safety of Caen's fortifications.

After Val-ès-Dunes William was securely back in control of the duchy of Normandy, though this hardly meant that he was always at peace with his nobles or his neighbours. In 1052, having just returned from England (a journey to be discussed below), William learned that the support of the king of France had flipped: not only did Henry I no longer support him as duke of Normandy, but he was also actively building a coalition of neighbouring lords to invade his duchy. By the end of 1052, armies led by Odo, brother of the king, Renaud, count of Clermont, and Guy, count of Ponthieu, had invaded Normandy on the north-eastern and eastern sides, with King Henry and Geoffrey Martel, count of Anjou and Maine, attacking from the south. These were generally small raids, burning and plundering, rather than full-scale attempts at military conquest; initially no battles were fought nor cities besieged. In response, William rushed here and there throughout the duchy, but he was unable to track down any attacking army before it had left the area.

In this struggle, William was increasingly aided by his Norman nobles, none of whom joined the king's side or rose up against the duke. At last, some of these, Robert, count of Eu, Hugh of Gournay, Walter Giffard, Roger of Mortemer and William de Warenne, caught up with the king's forces and defeated them – first at a skirmish near Saint-Aubin in 1053 and then at the Battle of Mortemer in 1054. Little is known about these conflicts, including their specific dates or places – although tradition places the latter near Mortemer Castle. William of Jumièges, our only source for both conflicts, says only that the battle was fought from dawn to noon and that the French fled from the battlefield. He further contends that 'the greater part of the French nobility was slain', and that this brought an end to the war, as Henry and the rest of the French invaders quickly left the duchy. Only one did not: Guy of Ponthieu, who would be imprisoned for two years until he swore fealty to William. As depicted in the Bayeux Tapestry, it would be this Guy who supposedly captured Harold Godwinson in 1065 and delivered him to William, after which Harold swore on relics that he would support William's inheritance of the crown of England. Although Guy did not accompany William on his invasion of England, his brother, Hugh, did; according to Guy of Amiens, Hugh directly participated in the slaying of Harold at the Battle of Hastings.

William had been absent from the battles of Saint-Aubin and Mortemer. No doubt he heard about how the Normans achieved victory over the previously more-vaunted French army. He also learned that victories in battle, no matter how significant the defeat, were rarely decisive. This would be proven in 1057 when King Henry I and Geoffrey of Anjou once again invaded Normandy. The French purpose was to capture Caen and Bayeux. Not knowing this, William gathered his army near Falaise and waited to see how the invasion progressed. William knew his land, but the king and Geoffrey did not: when the French tried to cross one of the estuaries of the Dives River, but could only get half across before the rising tide flooded the ford, William swept down onto their divided and disorganized forces. The soldiers who had not crossed the ford were attacked, and the rest of the French were unable to help them until the tide receded. By then it was too late, their comrades having already fled from the battlefield. Again, details are scant in contemporary sources, although we do know that the battle was fought in August 1057 at the fording of the estuary near Varaville. Later chronicles suggest that William massacred those he encountered, but contemporaries only record William's victory. It was the second victory in which he had been in command and the third for his Norman troops.

Henry and Geoffrey both escaped from Varaville, but they would not escape punishment for entering Normandy for military conquest. Before the year was out, William led an invasion of Maine, although he retreated after raiding the county. Then, in 1058, he captured the French towns of Tillières-sur-Avre and Thimert. And, in 1059–60, he returned to Maine. In the meantime, Geoffrey Martel had fled to Paris and William replaced him with the previous count, Herbert II. When Herbert died in 1062 without an heir, William was named as count of Maine. He was now duke of Normandy and count of Maine.

William had one more military adventure before his conquest of England in 1066. This time, it involved his support for the rebellion of Rivallon I of Dol against Conan II, duke of Brittany. We know more about this than perhaps any other of William's wars, other than his conquest of England, because it is depicted in almost half of the Bayeux Tapestry. Early in 1065, according to the Tapestry's tale, Harold Godwinson literally sailed into the middle of this uprising, having been blown off course across the Channel. On his way to relieve the siege of Dol by Conan, William retrieved Harold from Guy of Ponthieu, who had captured the English earl. On route, the army travelled past Mont-Saint-Michel, where Harold, recognized for his strength, rescued two Norman soldiers mired in the quicksand that still surrounds Mont-Saint-Michel. Dol was then relieved, with William, Harold and Rivallon pursuing Conan to his castle at Dinan. Their attacks on the fortress were cut short, however, when Conan wisely surrendered – depicted in the Tapestry by his handing William the keys to the castle on the tip of a spear. Yet William would never bear the title duke of Brittany. After Conan died in 1066 (of poison placed on his gloves) the duchy passed to his sister, Hawise. William certainly *controlled* it, however, to the point that he recruited enough Breton cavalry to form an entire unit at Hastings.

Harold Godwinson saves Norman soldiers from the quicksand surrounding Mont-Saint-Michel, from the Bayeux Tapestry. (*Musée de la Tapisserie de Bayeux*)

In the midst of this military chaos, William sought the hand of Matilda, the daughter of the powerful Baldwin V, count of Flanders. According to William of Jumièges, it was Duke William who approached Baldwin in 1049 with the idea of marrying his daughter. William was an ambitious young duke, having just survived the first threat to his rule. He was obviously seeking a connection with a strong ally and Baldwin certainly fulfilled that need. Baldwin also saw profit by securing his south-eastern border and he quickly agreed to the marriage.

Negotiations completed, William and Matilda were set to be married that year. But if the two thought this wedding was to be peaceful, calm and easy, they would be sadly disappointed. At the Council of Reims in October, Pope Leo IX decreed that neither Baldwin nor William could participate in the marriage, threatening them with excommunication should they do so. It is unclear from the several contemporary sources reporting this why Leo opposed this marriage and modern historians have been unable to bring clarity to the question. Some hold to consanguinity as the cause, but while the same council cited consanguinity in excommunicating two important northern French lords, Eustace II of Boulogne and Ingelram, the son of Guy of Ponthieu, no such accusation is made against William and Matilda and no genealogical connection has been found to connect the two within seven generations. Other historians contend, on only the slimmest of circumstantial evidence, that Matilda had been previously married, but it shouldn't have mattered even if she was. Most think that disputes between Flanders and the Holy Roman Empire were the cause; Baldwin had begun his wars against Holy Roman Emperor Henry III that year and Pope Leo was Henry's cousin, beholden to him for the papacy.

Consanguinity

Throughout the Middle Ages, canon law forbade marriages within four degrees of kinship (known legally by the term *consanguinity*). This was rarely enforced on those of the lower classes, where the small populations of most agricultural-based communities made it difficult to adhere strictly to such rules without creating consequences for the workforce. For the urban classes and nobles the enforcement was stricter, but there were always dispensations that could be acquired for some act of piety, like the patronizing of chapels or the constructions of ecclesiastical buildings. The profit gained from these dispensations is why some have suggested that the Catholic Church raised the prohibition to *seven* degrees in the ninth century. Less cynically, it may have been a simple recognition that the pool of nobility needed to increase, at least in the eyes of a Church that found it often easier to deal with regional lords than with the more powerful earls, counts, dukes, princes and kings. This resulted, at least initially, in the creation of more nobles overall and the advancing of lesser nobles to higher status. But it also created situations like that of William and Matilda where, even though they came from pretty different genealogical backgrounds, it was still difficult for them not to be related within seven generations (even if we can't reckon how exactly this would be). For a strict canonical observer of that law, as Pope Leo IX was – as evidenced by the number of marriages he annulled after becoming pope – the mere possibility of consanguinity may have been sufficient for him to forbid William and Matilda's marriage.

By the time of the Fourth Lateran Council in 1215, the Church recognized that the increased number of consanguineous degrees had produced more problems than it solved and the seven degrees was decreased once again to four.

Whatever the reason for Leo's objection, William and Matilda were married by 1056. If it happened before Leo's death in 1054, the union was in defiance of the Pope's decree. Regardless, the marriage was not fully sanctioned until the papacy of Nicholas II (1059–61), who agreed to it in exchange for William building two monasteries in Caen: the abbeys of 'aux-hommes' (for men) and 'aux-dames' (for women).

After the marriage, Baldwin and William became the closest of allies. In 1066, when William was planning the conquest of England, he approached the count of Flanders for assistance. Although Baldwin did not participate directly in the conquest of England – he was then 54 – he gave William useful advice and allowed him to recruit many Flemish soldiers for the battle. The duke of Normandy was able to recruit many Flemish subjects who saw the conquest of England as an opportunity to gain power and lands.

William's Claim on the English Throne
Up to 1057, William's military career had been defensive. Only when he had secured Normandy did it become offensive as he began to expand his lands and influence – into Maine, the Ile-de-France and Brittany. Expansionism might explain why William decided to attack further into France, especially with a powerful father-in-law to protect his eastern flank. But England? What possible reason did the duke of Normandy have to expand across the Channel into England, rather than direct further military excursions against France?

As we have already seen, the connections between Normandy and England were complicated before the conquest of 1066. Most historians point to the 1002 marriage of Duke Richard II's sister, Emma, to Athelred 'the Unready', the king of England, as the earliest initial link. Athelred used this marriage to provide a Norman location of exile: first in 1013, when he was defeated by Danish King Sweyn Forkbeard, and then again in 1016 when he was defeated by Sweyn's son, Cnut. Athelred died in 1016 and Emma then married Cnut – to create one of the strangest marriage triangles in history. She herself remained in England with her new husband and king, but she sent her two sons by Athelred, Edward and Alfred, to Normandy for 'safe-keeping'. Cnut died in 1035, with his eldest son, Harold I 'Harefoot' – not by Emma – becoming king of England and his second son, Harthacnut – by Emma – becoming king of Denmark. When Harold I died suddenly in 1040, Harthacnut became king of both England and Denmark. And when Harthacnut died two years later, Athelred and Emma's eldest son, Edward 'the Confessor', was named as king of England.

Such a dysfunctional royal family awaits its television series – but the point of it all was, at least for William's claim to the English throne, that he was Edward the Confessor's first cousin once removed. And, no doubt more importantly for the two lords' relationships, they had grown up in Normandy together – although as Edward was more than 20 years older than William and the duke was no more than 14 when Edward took over his kingdom, it is hard to know what kind of relationship had formed between them.

The story later told by the Normans is that William was in England in 1051, at a time when the king was having problems with the Godwins, the family of his queen, Edith. The duke was gone by their return to England in 1052, but from that early visit arose the idea that the childless Edward – who had placed Edith in a nunnery with seemingly no intention for divorce or procreation while her father and brothers were in exile – had named William his heir.

Edward proved unable to withstand the Godwin family's return for long. Less than a year after their exile, they were back in England. There was no direct military action – the Godwins came back with soldiers, but they did not have to fight to regain their positions. The English populace seemed in favour of the return of the earl of Wessex and his family. Edward clearly did not want them back, but he could not do anything to stop them.

Edward lost most of his power to Godwin and his family after their return and not even the earl's death the following year, in 1053, could bring it back. By 1060, the Godwinsons had secured control over all the earldoms of England, except for Mercia and, after Harold and Tostig Godwinsons' successful invasion of Wales in 1063, even Mercia could not stand in opposition to their power, especially that of Harold, who was earl of Wessex and 'chief minister' to Edward. Still, the Norman chroniclers and the Bayeux Tapestry insist that the Godwin family recognized William's right to inherit the English crown, as these portray Harold Godwinson swearing an oath in Normandy, in the presence of sacred relics, to support him.

The circumstances of this oath – not to mention the oath itself – are much in question. The Norman sources insist that Harold made an unexpected visit to Normandy in late 1064 or early 1065, though they disagree on how and why. One source says he was on a fishing trip gone awry. Another says he was on his way to Flanders when a storm blew him off course. One way or another, he came ashore in Ponthieu – where he fell into the hands of its count. When William heard of it, he took possession of the stranded earl. According to the Norman stories, Harold stayed in the Norman court for many weeks, during which he assisted William in his campaign to defend the city of Dol against Conan II of Brittany and might even have been knighted. Most importantly given what was to come, he was said to have given an oath that he would support William's claim to the throne of England. In some tellings, this agreement also included an arrangement of marriages: Harold would marry one of William's daughters and when the time came Harold's sister (who would then be the widow of the former king) would marry one of William's most powerful lords.

Contemporary English sources don't confirm much at all about such an agreement – or even a trip by Harold to Normandy – though the anonymous author of the *Vita Edwardi Regis*, written for his sister, Queen Edith, suggests that Harold was, in character, a man who took 'too many oaths'. The comment is made in relation to an oath Harold makes and breaks with his brother, Tostig, and not on Harold's visit to Normandy – which is otherwise not mentioned – but that hasn't prevented some scholars from seeing this as an indirect admission that at some point Harold had somewhere promised something to William. For the Normans, though, in their stories of the Conquest there was no question: a broken oath of fealty made for an accusation of treason by William against Harold when the earl of Wessex did not step aside to allow the duke of Normandy to take the kingship after Edward the Confessor died on 5 January 1066.

If Edward had indeed promised the throne to William back in 1051–2, then it should be said that he too apparently broke his word: the dying king recognized Harold as his heir just before he died. A few sources would try to question whether this actually happened, but it's difficult to deny the event when even the pro-Norman Bayeux Tapestry has Edward pointing at Harold when asked about

Harold makes his oath to support William's claim to the English throne, from the Bayeux Tapestry. (*Musée de la Tapisserie de Bayeux*)

his successor. And all the English sources indicate that the council of English nobles, the *witena-gemot*, met the day afterwards and immediately chose Harold as king, crowning him without delay. For the English, it didn't matter what, if anything, had been promised earlier. Edward had, in the end, chosen Harold.

News of Harold's coronation reached William quickly. The Bayeux Tapestry shows him preparing for war immediately. However, according to other sources, he took some time to decide if it was worth conquering England, possibly several weeks. William of Poitiers claims that the duke ultimately gave himself a year to invade the island kingdom. He consulted with his nobles and councils, no doubt ascertaining if he had military and economic support.

According to the Norman sources, Duke William also sent an embassy to Pope Alexander II requesting his approval of the invasion. Alexander, apparently convinced by stories of broken promises, answered by sending a banner to be carried into battle against the English. William of Poitiers has the matter agreed to quickly; William of Malmesbury and Orderic Vitalis have it taking longer. It is hard to know when such a mission was undertaken – the

Feudalism and Military Obligation

Throughout the Middle Ages, military obligation was traditionally based on what has been called feudalism. Military service was owed by vassals – land-holders, including ecclesiastical land-holders – to their lords for granting them these lands or fiefs. There was no uniformity in these obligations. Terms of feudal responsibilities differed with nearly every contract made between lord and vassal. For example, in medieval Romania, service was given until the age of 60, unless replaced by a suitable heir before then, four months of the year spent in castle duty, four months spent in the field and four months at home; and in the Latin kingdom of Jerusalem, military service was for the entire year or until one died. Outside of these more embattled regions, however, feudal military service was much shorter, usually being required only in defensive situations or when the lord who was owed the obligation desired to go on campaign. Under a particularly bellicose leader, this might mean a military service which could last much of the year for many years in a row, while under a more peaceful one, there was a likelihood of never being required to perform military duties.

When mustered, the medieval soldier was required to bring himself and his retinue and to pay for almost all of the arms, armour and provisions needed to sustain them on their campaign or in their fortification. If obligated for cavalry service, they were required to bring their horse. Ideally, this meant that no paid medieval army was needed. In reality, to fill out their numbers, most medieval military leaders were required to make promises of financial support or reimbursement for lost revenues or animals to those called into service. Even this did not always work, as there were a number of 'loopholes' that could be used to avoid one's obligations. For example, in 1300, when King Edward I of England called his feudal levy to military service, only forty knights and 366 sergeants responded; others cited fatigue, injury, illness and impoverishment, if they bothered to give an excuse at all, for avoiding their obligation.

dates of its departure from and return to Normandy are unknown – but it probably needed to have been early in the year, especially if, as some have suggested, William did not decide to undertake the invasion until he had papal justification.

Winter had to pass before supplies could be gathered efficiently. The duke could not starve his people to invade immediately, even if he was promising them substantial returns. However, winter did not keep the duke from other tasks, particularly the raising of an army. Once his nobles and council had given their support, William sent out a call to muster his troops.

In this William fared very well. He seems to have criss-crossed his duchy seeking soldiers, nobles of all ranks and their retinues – especially cavalry. From chronicles and charters we know a few of the places he visited: Fécamp, Rouen, Bonneville-sur-Touques, Caen and Bayeux. Most of his recruits would come from Normandy and Maine, but many also came from William's allies. The Boulognese came in quite healthy numbers, led by their count, Eustace II. William may also have waited until he learned that his father-in-law, Baldwin V, chose not to send an 'official' army, although Baldwin is said not to have kept Flemish soldiers from joining the expedition. Several Breton nobles and their soldiers, also allies to the Normans, arrived as well.

William was, no doubt, also gathering money to support his venture. Waging war was always an expensive task. In premodern Europe it was even more expensive if one was to wage war a long distance away; when troopships, horse-transports and supply vessels were required, the costs rose quickly. It was important that an invader consider whether the potential profits of such a venture would be sufficient to cover the losses of mounting the expedition. For William and those who financially supported him, the answer was clearly yes.

William had selected the Dives River and its numerous estuaries as the initial assembly point for men, supplies and the ships he would need to get them all to England. How many of these ships were built especially for this invasion is not known. The Bayeux Tapestry shows the construction of at least *some* of the fleet's ships: trees being felled; planks being planed; hulls being shaped, both inside and out. The shipwrights use axes and drills precisely as archaeological evidence shows that Northern ships were made – sawing wood dries out the core, leaving planks less flexible than those cut and shaped by axes. The finished vessels are shown tied to the shore and, later, sailing across the Channel. These ships serve different purposes – troop

Logistics in Medieval Warfare

The old but truthful adage that 'an army marches on its stomach' is often forgotten by premodern military historians who are as enamoured about the 'blood and guts' of warfare as are the narrative sources they frequently consult. The problem is a lack of evidence. The logistics of early modern and modern armies have numerous documents to collect evidence from, largely because the supplies for these armies – victuals, transports, arms and armour, horses and men – all needed to be paid for. Muster rolls are available for some later medieval armies – especially as feudal levies were being replaced by paid soldiers – and there are a few lists of arms and armour, but little else. And in earlier periods, like the eleventh century, there is virtually nothing. Some historians have resorted to guesses using calculations based on how much one might march or ride in a day, how much caloric intake a soldier or horse might need on campaign and even how much urine and defecation would be produced daily – and what all this waste might do to contaminate a water supply if deposited too near to a camp or siege site. Unfortunately, such guesswork is usually based on modern examples, with little regard to the forensic archaeology that has shown that premodern ideals of strength and physicality are vastly different than our own.

transports, horse transports and supply ships – but all are depicted as the same: clinker-built hulls; single side-post rudders; masts with single square sails, although the visible rowlocks in the top railing of the hull show they could be rowed – at sea those are covered by the kite-shaped shields of the soldiers aboard anchored into them. Most have dragons' heads or other effigies attached to their prows and three have standards on their masts.

The Bayeux Tapestry also shows the gathering of supplies, primarily arms and armour. Two servants carry the armour of an apparently well-to-do soldier on a rod: the suit of mail is draped from the arms, its coif distinctly folded down in a square attached to the neck, with a nasal spangenhelm rising above the rod at the neck of the suit and a sword dangling from the rod. In his left hand

Ships being built for the Norman fleet, from the Bayeux Tapestry. (*Musée de la Tapisserie de Bayeux*)

the forward servant carries a lance and possibly a second helm, grasped by its nasal; his right hand holds the rod onto his shoulders. The rear servant holds onto the rod with both hands. Two more servants drag further lances and nasal helmets on a four-wheeled cart along with a large tun of water or wine. The servants seem tremendously burdened, as they are shown bent over under the strain of pulling the cart. One uses a walking stick. More servants are carrying bags on their shoulders, likely foodstuffs, with one also carrying an axe. While the Bayeux Tapestry, confirmed by all contemporary sources, shows the Normans raiding the countryside as soon as they landed in England, William and his men would have known that they needed to travel with foodstuffs sufficient to last at least a few days.

In July William moved his fleet from the Dives to the Somme River. The most frequent reason given for this is that he was seeking for a safer harbour for a fleet that had grown to around 1,000 ships. The weather in the English Channel can be rough anytime during the year. Perhaps a larger river mouth, with two harbours on either side at Saint-Valéry-sur-Somme and across the river at Le Crotoy, might provide more safety for a large number of ships until favourable winds would allow them to cross with less risk. And we do know that weather was a problem – William would lose a number of ships in storms that hit his fleet as they moved from the Dives to the Somme.

The Norman fleet sails across the English Channel towards Pevensey, from the Bayeux Tapestry. (*Musée de la Tapisserie de Bayeux*)

But there are additional reasons why William might have moved to the Somme. In May an English spy was caught near the Dives while the fleet was being built, troops mustered and supplies gathered. He revealed that Harold Godwinson had the English army directly across from the Dives on the Isle of Wight and along the coasts nearby, anticipating the arrival there of the Normans. Making an amphibious attack on a beach has always been difficult. The D-Day landings will always be remembered for their difficulty and brutality. These were successful, but only because of the tenacity of the attacking forces. But 2,000 years before, two amphibious landings in England were attempted by Julius Caesar. Both failed, as they were unable to overcome the dogged defence of those on shore. By moving his fleet, William might have tried to avoid the same result as Caesar.

Another possibility is that William moved his fleet to gather the last of his men and supplies. Although the chronology is difficult to

Men carry the armour of a Norman soldier, from the Bayeux Tapestry. (*Musée de la Tapisserie de Bayeux*)

pinpoint, it is possible that William's Flemish, Boulognese and Upper Norman allies did not join him until after he had moved to Saint-Valéry. The Dives is not a large river and it simply may not have been sufficient in size to hold the number of ships William needed to make the crossing to England.

Norman chroniclers report that William became very impatient while waiting for the weather to change, for a 'favourable wind' to rise. Throughout July, August and almost all of September he was unable to move. It is not known if William heard of Harald Hardrada's invasion, though it is doubtful. His spies were as active in England as Harold's had been in Normandy, but they were focused on the southern coast and might not necessarily have information on what was happening in the north. Facing the same weather on the Channel as the duke of Normandy, the English king had allowed his troops first to return home – only to have to muster them quickly to march to face the Norwegian invader. Even if he *did*

The mouth of the River Somme, viewed from Saint-Valery towards La Crotoy. (*Kelly DeVries*)

know that the Norwegians had invaded or that this was the reason Harold had left the south, William could not possibly have known that the English king had defeated Harald Hardrada at Stamford Bridge only two days before he travelled from Saint-Valéry across the Channel on 27–28 September.

TOUR ONE: ORIGINS OF THE CONQUEROR

Falaise

A large bronze equestrian statue of William the Conqueror greets the visitor to the Centre d'Ville of Falaise, the birthplace of the Norman duke who would conquer England. It was raised on 26 October 1851 to celebrate the bastard child born in the city who would become one of the most famous men in world history. Dressed less as portrayed in the Bayeux Tapestry and more as a later medieval warrior-king, William is distinguished by his holding aloft the gonfanon given him by Pope Alexander II. On 19 September 1875, six more statues of the dukes of Normandy were erected in the square surrounding him; all seem to give obeisance to this favourite son of the city and the duchy.

From William's statue, one can see the stunning Château de Falaise (Castle of Falaise) (entrance fee required). It is on this spot, in a since-destroyed castle built by William's grandfather, that William was born.

Falaise Castle. (*Kelly DeVries*)

His father, Robert, had wrested control of the castle from his brother, Richard II, during the sibling rivalry before Richard died and Robert became duke. Unfortunately, only a small part of that earliest castle can be seen; in 1123 King Henry I (William's son) replaced it with the large, awe-inspiring keep that can still be seen today. This present castle is one of the most impressive, but unappreciated constructions of its time. It was here in 1174 that the Treaty of Falaise was signed, with the captive King William I of Scotland recognizing the lordship of the English King Henry II; and it was here too where Arthur, duke of Brittany, was held prisoner by his uncle, John, who had defeated him in 1202. John had ordered Arthur mutilated, but Hugh de Burgh, the castellan, refused to so and Arthur instead died in Rouen during the following year.

Only a smaller keep had been added to the castle between Henry II's construction and the capture of the castle and town by King Philip II Augustus in 1204. Three years later Philip added one of his customary tall cylindrical keeps to the site, extending its protection and ability to house a large garrison. Strangely, this tower carries the name Talbot's Tower, after John Lord Talbot who occupied the site during much of the fifteenth century. It was also Talbot who repaired the castle and added numerous gunports to the walls and towers of the castle in an attempt to defend the castle from early gunpowder weapons. These were not needed, however, when King Charles VII captured the castle without needing to besiege it during his reconquest of Normandy in 1449–50.

The city saw heavy fighting during the Second World War. In 1944, regrouped Nazi forces tried to halt the Allied troops who had come ashore on the beaches of Brittany and Normandy a few months before here, in what became known as the Falaise Pocket (or Gap). Two-thirds of the city was destroyed, but the castle and William's statue remained largely untouched.

Caen

Shortly after his marriage to Matilda, William moved his capital to Caen. Although it had been associated with the Norman dukes since they developed the small Roman town into a medieval city in 912, from this point forward the city would be identified with the footprint of the Conqueror.

Caen Castle. (*Kelly DeVries*)

Among the several sites connected to William and Matilda are the two monastic establishments they established as penance for their marriage. One, 'aux-hommes' (for men), was begun with the building of a church dedicated to Saint-Étienne (Stephen) in 1063.

Saint-Etienne Church in Caen.

The stone marking the burial place of William the Conqueror. (*Kelly DeVries*)

The abbey followed three years later, dedicated shortly before the Norman invasion army and fleet moved to the Somme River.

William would be interred there following his death in Rouen in 1087, under a large black marble slab. He would not remain there in peace, however. During the Wars of Religion in 1562, William's body was disinterred, his bones scattered and his marble tombstone destroyed. Only a thigh bone was found, which was reinterred in 1642. New tombstones were placed in 1742 and, after they were destroyed again, during the nineteenth century after the French Revolution. Today this site is marked by a white marble slab with no decoration other than a Latin epitaph: '*Hic sepultus est Invictissimus Guillelmus conquestor, Normanniae Dux, et Angliae Rex, hujusce domus conditor, qui obit anno MLXXXVII*' ('Here lies the most invincible William the Conqueror, Duke of Normandy, King of England, the founder of this house, who died in 1087'). Saint-Étienne originated as a Romanesque construction, its apse replaced by Gothic structures in 1120 and again in 1166. The nine external towers and spires were added in the thirteenth century. Although the church was damaged during the Wars of Religion and French Revolution, the church has been restored to its medieval glory.

Saint-Trinité Church in Caen.

The Abbaye-aux-Dames began similarly to its male counterpart, with its church dedicated to the Sainte-Trinité (Holy Trinity) around the same time. Duchess Matilda took a particular interest in this establishment and added a nunnery to which she gave her eldest daughter by William, Cecilia, in 1066. Matilda would be buried in the choir of Sainte-Trinité in 1083, under a similar black marble slab as her husband would be four years later. But, while William's would not last beyond the sixteenth century, Matilda's still lies over her grave, which has been undisturbed. Her gravemarker also contains a longer Latin epitaph:

> *Egregie pulchri tegit haec structura sepulchri*
> *Moribus insignem, germen regale, Mathildem.*
> *Dux Flanditra pater huic extitit, Adala mater,*
> *Francorum gentis Roberti filia regis*
> *Et soro Hnrici, regali sede potiti,*

Regi magifico Willelmo juncta marito,
Praesentem sedem recenter fecit et aedem,
Tum multis terris quam multis rebus honestis
A se ditatam, se procurante dicatem.
Haec consolatrix inopum, pietatis amatrix,
Gazis dispersis, pauper sibi, dives egenis.
Sic infinitae petiit consortia vitae.
In prima mensis, post primam, luce novembis.

('This sepulchre of remarkable beauty covers Matilda, noble in character, a royal scion. The Count of Flanders was her father, Adele her mother, daughter of Robert, king of the French and sister of Henry, possessor of the royal throne. She was married to the magnificent king, William and lately built this church which she piously built and consecrated. The comforter, tender lover, of the poor. Wealth dispersed, the needy rich but rich to the unfortunate. Thus she sought the fellowship of eternal life on the second day of November'.)

Her daughter, Cecilia, would also be buried in the church in 1126, a resident of the nunnery for more than 60 years. She was not interred near her mother and her grave has not been located. Sainte-Trinité also began as a Romanesque structure, though a Gothic vault was added in 1130. It too was damaged during the French Revolution, but later restored. Both churches can be visited without charge during daylight hours.

Saint-Étienne lies to the west of the castle and Sainte-Trinité to the east. William started the construction on the castle around 1060, but only a central keep was completed by the time of his death. When in Caen following the English conquest, William and his family would stay in this keep. It was destroyed by William's son, Henry I, who replaced it with a much larger keep, around 1123. The foundation of William's keep has been excavated and can be seen by a visitor (a fee is required for entry to the castle). Henry also built a large hall for the court and a church dedicated to Saint George. All of Henry's buildings still exist, although some have been vastly reconstructed.

In 1182, the English King Henry II held a court in the Caen Castle with his sons, Richard the Lionheart and John – in an effort (apparently in vain) to sort out their differences. These Angevin kings were responsible for building the initial stone walls around the castle – these may have been preceded by earthen walls and a wooden palisade. A large barbican in front of the gate was also added during the Middle Ages, although exactly when is unknown. And in 1204, the French King Philip II Augustus acquired it during his conquest of Normandy following his return from the Third Crusade. It also became a focal point of Hundred Years War fighting in 1346, 1417 and 1450. Following Henry V's conquest in 1417, the stone walls were rebuilt, with gunports and other anti-gunpowder artillery devices added, including an oddly shaped artillery tower on the northern side. It sustained damage during the French Revolution in 1793 and by bombardment by Allied forces liberating Normandy in 1944.

Archaeological excavations continue at the castle, which is owned by the city, and so far have revealed the remains of cellars, a smokehouse, a powder house and a forge (the last dating to the fourteenth century). Located within the castle today is the Museé de Beaux-Artes and the Museé de Normandie. The latter is filled with medieval artefacts found in the castle and city.

Also medieval in Caen is the Church of Saint-Pierre (St. Peter), built between the thirteenth and sixteenth centuries, which effectively became the 'cathedral' of the city following its construction. Its spire was destroyed in 1944 but was rebuilt. A few wooden houses dated to the Middle Ages have also survived the various military destructions of the millennium since William and Matilda lived in the city.

Bayeux

Bayeux was the ecclesiastical capital of Normandy during William the Conqueror's lifetime, with his half-brother, Odo, serving as bishop during and after the invasion. If, as is depicted on the Bayeux Tapestry, Harold Godwinson took an oath on sacred relics to support William's inheritance of the English throne, it may have been here. Bayeux is one of the oldest cities in this part of France, with a Roman development of the Celtic town sometime after Julius Caesar conquered Gaul in the first century AD. The Romans called it Augustodorum and by the end of the third century it was walled – these would be removed in the eighteenth century – and had grown

Bayeux Church.
(*Kelly DeVries*)

substantially, especially with the resettlement of the Suevi sometime during the Roman occupation. The Vikings raided it several times during the ninth and tenth centuries, settling in the city during the final century. One commentator reported that the inhabitants spoke Danish before the Normans took over.

In 1077, following his participation in the Norman Conquest, Odo replaced the church where Harold may have taken his oath with a larger Romanesque structure – on 14 July it was dedicated in the presence of William the Conqueror. But it, together with much of the city, was burned by William's son, Henry I, in his usurpation of the Norman duchy from his brother, Robert II of Normandy, who had newly returned from the First Crusade. (Pope Urban II had promised the First Crusaders that their positions and land-holdings would be secure, but he was dead when Robert and the other First Crusaders returned home and Henry seems to have conveniently forgotten this papal promise.) The city was again raided several times during the Hundred Years War before being finally captured by the French King Charles VII following his victory over the English at the Battle of Formigny in 1450, which was fought nearby.

Following Charles' recapture of Bayeux, a new cathedral dedicated to Notre Dame (Our Lady) was built; it was mostly reconstructed during the nineteenth century. What is more important is what had been kept in that church from at least 1476 – when it is first recorded being there – although probably for much longer: the Bayeux Tapestry. It is not actually a tapestry per se, but an embroidery; however, it has been known as a 'tapestry' since at least 1729 when it was removed from the church and placed in the Museé de la Tapisserie de Bayeux. It was at this time that a linen backing was sewn onto the tapestry, a poor decision that unfortunately now cannot be undone as it would ruin the embroidery. Various incarnations of the museum have existed, including the present one, in which inside visitors can view the extraordinary Bayeux Tapestry today. This remarkable artefact measures 230ft (70m) long and 20in (50cm) wide and it presents seventy scenes related to the Norman Conquest (although more may have been lost over time), many of them shown in this book, in addition to margins added above and below the main scenes that often contain what seem to be completely unrelated material. It has been accurately dated to around the year 1070, but who commissioned it and who wove it are unknown. Odo is most frequently suggested as the commissioner – although other candidates are Queen Emma, Edward the Confessor's widow, Matilda, William's wife, or Adela, William and Matilda's daughter. The weavers were either English (from Kent), Norman (from Bayeux), French (from the Abbey of Saint-Florent de Saumur in the Loire Valley) or Breton (from Mont-Saint-Michel).

That the Bayeux Tapestry, this beautiful anomalous depiction of medieval warfare, has survived the Wars of Religion, French Revolution and the Second World War – Heinrich Himmler wanted it for his own collection – is truly miraculous.

Fécamp

Another ecclesiastical site of importance for William was the Norman Abbey of Fécamp. By the eleventh century, this abbey already had a long history. Founded as a nunnery in 658, it was destroyed by Vikings in 842. The church was rebuilt by Duke Richard I and the monastery refounded by his son, Richard II. In 1001 this second Richard brought Guglielmo da Volpiano from Italy to give the Benedictine monks order and importance. (Both Richards and Guglielmo were buried there.) Fécamp had connections well before William's conquest. King Cnut had granted the abbey large amounts of land in the south of England, with Edward the Confessor adding the royal minster

Fécamp Abbey.

church in Steyning and its immense holdings in 1047. After his exile Godwin took Steyning for himself and it passed on to his son, Harold, after his death. Thus there was no questioning of Fécamp's support of William's war against Harold. In gratitude for this support William would return Steyning, also adding several more lands following his victory. Unfortunately, none of the eleventh-century Norman construction remains, although the abbey church dedicated to the Holy Trinity, built between 1175 and 1220, is worth a visit.

Dol and Dinan

Most other places in Normandy that were important to the history of William are unknown or have completely changed. Of the scenes from the Bayeux Tapestry, the motte-and-bailey castles at Dol and Dinan have been destroyed or, at least, not located. The castle at Dol seems to have stood until at least 1173 when it was besieged and captured by Hugh de Kevelioc, earl of Chester, in his revolt against King Henry II – who recaptured it in 1174. It may have been taken down shortly afterwards, as it does not have a place in the capture of Dol in 1204 by Guy of Thouars on behalf of Philip II Augustus.

The Siege of Dol, from the Bayeux Tapestry. (*Musée de la Tapisserie de Bayeux*)

The Motte-and-Bailey Castle

One of the most effective, easily and quickly built fortifications, the motte-and-bailey castle, was used by William the Conqueror during and after his invasion of England. Simply described, the motte part of the motte-and-bailey castle was a mound made of earth topped by a superstructure of timber. The bailey was a yard enclosed by an earthen rampart – at times topped with a wooden palisade – that surrounded the motte and was usually separated from it by a wide and deep ditch. Usually a ditch also surrounded the bailey. As such, the motte-and-bailey castle provided protection for its inhabitants by the rampart, the size of the bailey, the depth and width of its ditches and the height of the mound.

Remains of motte-and-bailey castles have been found throughout northern Europe – where the soil is heavy enough to allow construction of a steep hill – dating to the tenth and eleventh centuries. However, in England the first did not appear until the 1050s, when three were built along the Welsh border by Normans who visited his court at the time of the Godwin family exile: Hereford, Ewyas Harold and Richard's Castle.

Before his conquest of England, William the Conqueror knew the value of the motte-and-bailey castle, as he had built a number of these in the eastern part of his duchy (where he resided), in the western part (where he had to fight some of his nobles for power) and in the County of Maine. It was no surprise, then, that William also used motte-and-bailey castles in his conquest of England. Shortly after landing, it appears he built one in the town of Hastings – one is shown being constructed in the Bayeux Tapestry. Following his defeat of Harold, he built several more throughout the kingdom. In these he could garrison a few men, from which they could give military aid when rebellions rose up against the new king's rule.

An example of such troubles took place in the town of York. Beginning in 1068 the citizens began a series of revolts against their Norman rulers. William answered the first of these by building a motte-and-bailey castle at what would become known as Baile Hill. It was a particularly large fortress, with a garrison of more than

500 soldiers. Still, in early 1069, the inhabitants of York revolted once again, even attacking the castle that William had constructed to watch over them. It held out until William arrived with reinforcements and the uprising was put down. The king then constructed a second motte-and-bailey castle across the Ouse River from the first – what is now the motte below Clifford's Tower – building the fortification in eight days. But even this did not secure the town against rebellion. A few months later, in September 1069, the citizens of York, aided by some Danish mercenaries, again rose against Norman rule and again they attacked the castles. On this occasion the York rebels prevailed, capturing and burning the wooden superstructures of both castles. Again William was forced to come north with his army, severely punished the people and in 1070 the two motte-and-bailey castles were rebuilt. It was only then that the people submitted to their new king.

   Although it is not known how many were built during William's reign, between 500 and 1,000 are the numbers given by modern castellologists, making this quite likely the most extensive and rapid fortification building program in history. Even before William died, it had become apparent that motte-and-bailey castles would be replaced, sometimes using the mottes as foundations, by stone castles. William himself built three of these, in London (the White Tower), Colchester and Richmond, with more following during the rule of his successors.

   At least until the Hundred Years War, Dinan had a much richer and more peaceful history, following its Bayeux Tapestry depiction. Where the motte-and-bailey castle was located is unknown, but it seems not to exist today. It may have been removed during the twelfth and thirteenth century when a stone castle and a circuit of walls were constructed. These still exist for the most part, although reconstructed in places and, during the fifteenth century, refitted with gunpowder artillery features: gunports and artillery towers. Outside of these walls in 1358, the French hero and later duke of Brittany, Bertrand du Guesclin, challenged any English besieger to a duel – Sir Thomas of answered and was defeated – as remembered by a bronze equestrian statue on site. Guesclin's heart is buried in

The keep of the castle at Dinan. (*Kelly DeVries*)

the Basilica of Saint-Sauveur (Holy Saviour), a lovely Romanesque church in Dinan (dating from the twelfth to the sixteenth century) – the rest of his body was interred in the Basilica of Saint-Denis next to the kings and queens of England. Also worth visiting in Dinan are the Church of Saint-Malo, the Clock Tower (both dating to 1490) and several medieval houses.

Mont-Saint-Michel

Mont-Saint-Michel is also depicted in the Bayeux Tapestry. One of the great treasures of medieval France, the Romanesque abbey that still in large part exists today was under construction when William and Harold passed by, which may explain the oblong construction seen

The Siege of Dinan, from the Bayeux Tapestry. (*Musée de la Tapisserie de Bayeux*)

on the Tapestry. Over the centuries, this monastery and its church was frequently rebuilt and restored; a circuit of walls were added. These were strong enough to resist an English siege that lasted from 1423 to 1434 – although the most intense fighting took place in 1423–4 and 1433–4. Walking through the beautiful ancient streets and up the

Mont-St-Michel is not just an incredibly important historical site, but an incredibly beautiful one, too. (*Kelly DeVries*)

ancient stairs – for Mont-Saint-Michel has been an important site for much longer than its appearance in the Bayeux Tapestry – looking at the amazing medieval structures to the top levels of the monastery, it is difficult to imagine what William and Harold might have seen. But a walk around the island, and observing the signs warning against the quicksand still there, easily brings an image of Harold saving two of William's soldiers. No doubt those soldiers were among William's army when it defeated and killed their Mont-Saint-Michel saviour.

Dives

The three battlefields on which William or his supporters fought in Normandy before his conquest – Val-es-Dunes, Mortemer and Varaville – have not been accurately located. There is a sign marking a spot by the Dives River where the last battle is said to have been fought, but, as the river has changed over the past millennium, this cannot be ascertained until archaeological excavations prove otherwise.

The same can be said about where on the Dives River William originally gathered his forces and fleet. The Dives still runs into the English Channel and is navigable for about 24 miles (38km), although

The mouth of the River Dives.

there are currently no harbours along that route large enough to house the 1,000 vessels that William used to invade England. There is little doubt that the coast near and mouth of the river has changed.

Saint-Valery-sur-Somme
The mouth of the Somme River is much larger than the Dives today, just as it was in 1066, and Saint-Valery-sur-Somme still provides a substantial harbour for ships. Likely both coast and harbour have changed and nothing remains in the town from William's time. There is a modern monument commemorating William's conquest, however. It reads: '*De ce port Guillaume de Normandie partit a la*

The church and wall of Saint-Valery. (*Kelly DeVries*)

conquete de l'Angleterre 1066' ('From this port William of Normandy departed on his conquest of England, 1066'). The town is named for the monk Gualaric (Walric), who settled in the area in 611. The site was of strategic importance, so an abbey remained there until being destroyed by Vikings in the eighth and ninth centuries. The town survived and of course profited greatly from what William paid to support his army and fleet for the months he was there. By the time of the Hundred Years War Saint-Valery had reacquired the abbey – although it would be destroyed by the English when the town was captured – a circuit of walls and a nearby castle. The remnants of these can be seen throughout the town. Among these are several nicely preserved gates; the one named Porte Guillaume, leading to the beach at the mouth of the Somme, is especially important as it is through here that Joan of Arc was led by her English captors as they displayed her in a number of Norman towns on her way to her trial and execution in Rouen. A 'cell' in the medieval walls nearby is identified as her prison while in Saint-Valery, but this tradition is questionable. The heavily restored Abbey church is also worth a visit, although very little of the medieval structure remains.

Chapter 3

THE NORWEGIAN INVASION

Although none of the contemporary sources blame Harold for the exile of his brother at the end of 1065, Tostig hardly felt the same as he sailed away to the court of Flanders. He was 'angered at everyone', writes William of Malmesbury, but especially his brother.

We don't know how long Tostig stayed in Flanders, but he was probably still there a couple of months later, when Edward the Confessor died on 5 January 1066. It may only have been after Harold's coronation a few days later that Tostig started to seek for an ally to aid his return to England.

It might be tempting to envision a scenario in which Tostig had his eyes on the throne himself, but no contemporary source makes the suggestion. Even before he left England he'd surely known that the crown, if it went to a Godwinson, would go to his older brother. More likely, Tostig only wanted to return to England and recover his earldom. After all, the men that he asked for help were all themselves potential claimants to the newly-occupied throne.

Baldwin V of Flanders was backing his son-in-law, William of Normandy, and the medieval chronicler Orderic Vitalis – although his is the only source to say so – has Tostig approach the Norman duke first. Tostig told William that he would 'faithfully secure the crown for him if he would cross to England with a Norman army'. But William, it seems, had not yet decided to invade England. Tostig, impatient, left.

From here Tostig largely disappears from the English or Norman sources, though his journey is continued in Norwegian Kings' Sagas. Recorded between c.1180 and c.1230, five of these (one in Latin and four in Old Norse) report what happened in the next few months.

Sagas as Evidence

Old Norse sagas were the most prolific vernacular literature in the Middle Ages. They recount long and detailed narratives of godly or heroic deeds, often set in a context connected to historical events and people. Most seem to have originated as oral tales, likely composed contemporary or near contemporary to what they record, but were not written down until later, in the twelfth to the fourteenth century. Consequently, historians have been reluctant to use sagas as sources; that there are errors and embellishments when compared to more trustworthy sources justifies this reluctance. However, what if sagas are the only records, as they are for so much of the Norwegian invasion of England in 1066?

From Normandy Tostig travelled to Denmark to meet with King Sweyn II Estridsson. Tostig made the same promise to him that he had made to William: a crown for an army. Sweyn heard him out, but the Danish king – who as grandson of Sweyn Forkbeard, nephew of Cnut and cousin of Harthacnut was in direct line to the English throne – decided not to enforce his potential claim on the crown.

Tostig's next stop was Norway, where he met King Harald Hardrada. The saga writer Snorri Sturluson, in his *Heimskringla*, presents Tostig as being effusive in his praise: 'It is certain to everyone that no warrior had ever been born in Scandinavia equal to you', he writes. Again the former earl promised the English crown.

Harald's reaction was different from the others: 'King Harald considered carefully what the earl had said and realized that he said much truth; and besides he was eager to have this kingdom', Sturluson says. The men made plans. Harald began to gather his army and fleet, while Tostig returned to Flanders to gather his own retainers.

Orderic Vitalis says that Harald Hardrada needed six months to prepare for his invasion of England, meaning that Tostig must have reached Oslo by the beginning of March, some two months after his brother Harold Godwinson had been crowned king of England. This may seem a great distance, especially in the winter months, but it was hardly an impossibility or even a rarity for the people of the North Sea: Tostig would have been travelling with the wind largely

Did Tostig Visit Harald Hardrada?

Some historians, distrusting the Norse sagas, have suggested that Tostig made no visit to Harald Hardrada and didn't hear about the invasion until after it had been launched – perhaps from an Orkney Islands ally, Copsig, who is known to have joined his seventeen ships to Tostig's fleet, estimated to be between forty and forty-five ships, around the time that Tostig was on the southern coast of England. Believing this to be the best possibility for returning to his earldom, Tostig then left the Isle of Wight and sailed north to join the Norwegian king. This timeline has its difficulties, however: for one thing, it requires Tostig travelling to Wessex, then to Mercia and then to Northumbria to meet with a king he'd never met in order to join an invasion that was going forward with or without his help. For another thing, why indeed would Harald accept him as an ally without previous coordination?

at his back, avoiding adverse weather and the open sea by travelling along the coastlines of northern Europe and Scandinavia.

We next hear of Tostig on the south shore of England. According to the *Anglo-Saxon Chronicle*, it was sometime after 24 April that Tostig came to the Isle of Wight with ships and there gathered money and supplies before raiding the coastline to Sandwich. It's roughly 1,000 miles (1,600km) between Oslo and the Isle of Wight via Bruges and a Viking longship averaged 5–10 knots. Assuming the slowest average speed – he was, after all, running against predominant wind and current at a bad time of year – Tostig would have needed some 174 hours at sea to reach the Isle of Wight. A departure from Oslo by the middle of March would leave the former earl plenty of time to manage this, even accounting for his need to pick his way between early spring storms.

A number of factors must have influenced Tostig's decision to raid the Isle of Wight and the southern coast of England. For one thing, doing so was something of a Godwin family tradition: it was here that he, Harold and their father had united in 1052 to make their invasion/return from exile. Beyond this fact, Tostig had a manor on the island, in Nunwell – exactly the sort of place to gather money

The routes of Tostig's possible journeys around the North Sea in 1066. (*Michael Livingston*)

and materiel for the invasion that he knew was coming. At the same time, the island and the mainland around it belonged to the earl of Wessex and his brother had not named another to that title when he'd become king. An attack on Wessex lands was thus an attack not just on the kingdom, but on the king's very own holdings. (Harold, in fact, had a personal manor on the Isle of Wight at nearby Kern; though we have no record of it being specifically attacked by Tostig, it's hard to imagine it wasn't!)

In addition to getting his own supplies and making a personal affront to his brother, Tostig might also have hoped that raiding the southern coast would put Harold's defences on alert – on the opposite side of England from the place he and the Norwegian king were planning to invade. If a distracting feint was part of his plans, Tostig would have quickly realized that there was no need to draw Harold's eye to the south: across the Channel in Normandy, William had now made his own intentions clear. The English king was thus already gathering, as the *Anglo-Saxon Chronicle* reports, 'so many naval and land hosts' from the south of England 'that no king before had ever gathered so many'.

Tostig headed north, making a brief landing at Lindsey, before he reached Dunfermline in Scotland, where he was welcomed by the court of King Malcolm III. The former earl stayed there, according to the *Anglo-Saxon Chronicle*, through the summer.

The Norwegian Invasion of England

In the meantime, Harald Hardrada had mustered his invasion force. His fleet is recorded in the Norwegian Kings' Sagas as 250 ships in size, which would have held 11,000–12,000 soldiers, if estimates of 44–48 soldiers per vessel are accurate (calculated from the number that would have oared excavated Viking ships); others suggest that this figure of soldiers per vessel is too low and that his force was closer to 18,000. Using the same lower per ship estimation, Tostig might have added an extra 3,000 soldiers to the Norwegian force, although most historians, on no certain evidence, suggest he brought far fewer to the invasion.

Eleventh-century Ships

In Northern Europe at the end of the eighth century, the Vikings began to attack the lands across the sea from Scandinavia. These attacks were completely unanticipated, with the English scholar Alcuin writing to Athelred, the king of Northumbria, concerning the Viking raid on the Lindisfarne monastery in 793: 'never before has such terror appeared in Britain as we have suffered from a pagan race, nor was it thought that such an inroad from the sea could be made'. Fortunately, because archaeologists have excavated so many Viking ships, our knowledge of their construction and use at sea is substantial.

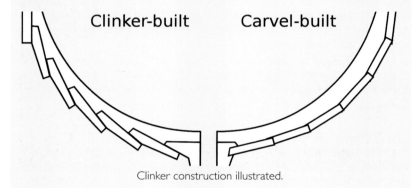

Clinker construction illustrated.

All are clinker-built vessels with strong keels onto which overlapping planks are attached and further secured by an interior skeleton of wooden staves and girders. These strong keels allowed a deeper, flatter and longer hull to be constructed. They also allowed the placement of a heavy mast, perhaps as long as 39ft (12m). Many ships took part in the Viking raids over the following centuries. They varied in size and, seemingly, in purpose. Some were quite large in length and width. Among those recovered by archaeologists, the Gokstad ship measures 75ft (23m) in length and 17ft (5.2m) in width; the Skuldelev 5-7 ship measures 92ft (28m) long (its width cannot be estimated because of the bad state of preservation). Both are shallow in depth, which suggests that they were built as warships.

Other ships were considerably smaller in length and width, but larger in depth, perhaps suggesting that they were vessels that would be used chiefly for transporting cargo. The Viking ship could be rowed, with the largest vessels equipped with fifteen or more rowlocks cut into both sides of the hull. It was also equipped with a large square sail, which would add considerable speed. A single rudder attached to one side near the stern steered the ship.

The Osberg ship, perhaps the finest extant Viking ship, was excavated from a burial mound in 1904–05. (*Kelly DeVries*)

England, France and the Holy Roman Empire soon replicated the design of the Viking ships, so that by the eleventh century, almost all Northern European were galleys equipped with large square sails. (The dendrochronology of Skuldelev 5-7 shows it to be of English wood, likely constructed there.) The Bayeux Tapestry shows that, while they were generally low-hulled, these ships could be altered to take on horses. Unfortunately, how this was done cannot be seen on the tapestry, nor from the excavated Viking vessels. Other horse-transports, however, show that the adding of stalls was not a particularly difficult alteration and that slings could be attached to these stalls in order to keep the horses stable while crossing rougher water.

A Norman ship carrying horses, from the Bayeux Tapestry. (*Musée de la Tapisserie de Bayeux*)

For the two invasions of England in 1066, large numbers of ships were used. Harald and Tostig's combined fleet contained more than 300 ships, while contemporary numbers vary between 696 and 3,000 for William the Conqueror's fleet. The difference in the size of fleets was largely due to William's need for a large number of horse-transports, as no more than ten horses could be safely carried on a single ship – Harald needed none of these – and the fact that Norwegians were accustomed to serving both as soldiers and sailors, while Normans were not.

After gathering his invasion army, ships and supplies, Harald sailed first to the Shetland Islands, in a direct route across the North Sea, and then to the Orkney Islands. These were part of the Kingdom of Norway at the time, so they were safe landings and points of resupply. They may also have added a few soldiers, although this would not have been many: the islands likely had a relatively small population, just as they do today. Harald next sailed to Dunfermline in Scotland, where he met Scottish King Malcolm III. Some Scots seem to have joined the Norwegians, but Malcolm did not, nor did he add his army to Harald's forces.

It is also in Scotland that some sources have Tostig joining Harald, though most place the meeting at the Tynemouth on 8 September, 'as previously planned', according to the *Anglo-Saxon Chronicle*. The entire invasion force then travelled south, along the Cleveland

The probable routes taken by Harald Hardrada (in brown, following the river) and Harold Godwinson (in green, following the Roman roads) to York and the Battle of Stamford Bridge. (*Michael Livingston*)

coast, landing periodically to plunder and take on fresh water. Only when they tried to attack the sizable town of Scarborough did the Norwegians meet any resistance. When that town's militia defended the beach, a group of Norwegians was forced to climb to the high ground above the city, where King John's castle stands today and a Roman signalling station had stood previously. From there, according to Snorri Sturluson, they threw flaming logs onto the city below, burning most of it to the ground.

The Norwegians did not land on the English coast again before sailing up the Humber River and into the Ouse River. They anchored the fleet at Ricall, about 10 miles (16km) south of York – the great city of the north, founded by Scandinavians and only a few generations earlier the seat of their power on the island.

The Battle of Fulford Gate

York was the target. And although Harald and Tostig could have followed the Ouse upstream into its heart, the Norwegian king wanted his army on the ground. Viking longships were marvels of nautical engineering. They could move fast on the rivers, far upstream of where defences might be expected. However, for all the advantage that Harald's ships might thus give him in a surprise attack, they could undoubtedly be a weakness if he found himself under threat while on the water. His ships, tightly packed with men, would be highly vulnerable to archery in particular.

And he had reason to worry.

His slow rate of travel during this phase – he anchored at Ricall on 20 September, twelve days after he met Tostig in the Tynemouth – had enabled him to reconnoitre the nearby lands. He undoubtedly had learned that Morkere and Edwin, the earls of Northumbria and Mercia, had gathered their troops in York, 'as great a force as they could from their earldoms' claims the *Anglo-Saxon Chronicle*. They had moved south out of York, putting themselves between the invaders and their goal at a place called Fulford Gate.

The English earls chose their field well. Taking a position at Fulford Gate enabled them to flank the river while they also blocked the road that Harald would use to approach. What's more, the site was a natural bottleneck: the road was narrowed by the Ouse on one side and a dike-fronted swamp on the other. It was an ideal position and Harald and Tostig had little choice but to try to dislodge them.

Surprisingly, the English and Norman sources give more detail on the Battle of Fulford Gate than they do on the more major conflict at Stamford Bridge a few days later. They tell us for certain that the Norwegians approached in a linear shield-wall formation. As they did so, Morkere, positioned on the dike side of the road surprised them by charging his own shield-wall into the Norwegian troops opposite him. These troops, in a remarkable coincidence, were commanded by Tostig, the earl he had replaced the year before. Tempting though it might be to imagine that this fact may have motivated his charge – surely if a movie is made of the battle, it will be – but in truth this was no doubt a tactic planned by both brothers: Morkere would charge where the Norwegians were likely to be weakest, hoping to put them to flight. If one wing of the army ran, so, too, might the rest of them.

It almost worked.

Tostig's troops did indeed flee, after Morkere's soldiers had 'laid low many', writes John of Worcester. But Harald's men didn't follow them. Instead, his fearless soldiers attacked Edwin's shield-wall in turn, quickly overrunning it before turning onto Morkere's forces, which were now trapped between them and Tostig's soldiers. What had seemed a clever tactic had failed. The invaders took some casualties in the fight, but the English army was almost completely destroyed. Hemmed in by the very landscape that had been their advantage, they had nowhere to flee. Many died in the river as they tried to escape the slaughter, while on the swamp side, the Norwegian Kings' Sagas report, 'the dead lay there so thick that the Norwegians could travel with dry feet over the swamp'.

Before Harald and Tostig could move much further, they received a message from the citizens of York – undoubtedly told of the Norwegians' victory by fleeing soldiers – wishing to negotiate the surrender of their city. Four days later, hostages were arranged – 150 from each side to be delivered the following day – and Harald and Tostig moved their troops to the nearby village of Stamford Bridge, north-east of York.

It was 24 September.

The Battle of Stamford Bridge

It can be safely asserted that King Harold Godwinson did not hear of the Norwegian invasion of Northumbria before 15 or 16 September. He was in London at the time, having withdrawn from the south once he concluded that the threat of another attack there by his brother or the launching of an invasion by William was unlikely. A ship brought the news to him, reporting both that Tostig and Harald Hardrada had joined forces and that their target was York – more than 200 miles (322km) away.

Harold mustered his troops very quickly; 15,000–18,000 men is the estimate. Many were huscarls, but most were fyrd.

The English Army in 1066

Although derided by William the Conqueror as a 'people devoid of military knowledge' (according to Henry of Huntingdon), the English army in 1066 was one of the best armed and most highly organized military forces of the Middle Ages.

They were divided into three types. The first and most formidable of these was the huscarls. They were well-armed professional soldiers who had been introduced to English service by Cnut when he ascended the throne in 1016. These were paid professionals, with Edward the Confessor instituting that their wages were to come directly from the treasuries of the king. This ensured their loyalty to the Crown. It is likely that there was no force in Europe equal to the English huscarls. They were well trained, able to use both the two-handed battleaxe and the sword with equal dexterity. Even the Norwegians

English soldiers, from the Bayeux Tapestry. (*Musée de la Tapisserie de Bayeux*)

had praise for these skilled soldiers, as Snorri Sturluson writes: 'They were men who were so valiant that one was a better soldier than two of the best of Harald [Hardrada]'s men.'

The second type of eleventh-century English soldiers was the fyrd. The fyrd was filled by the general levied militia. Since the very beginning of the Middle Ages, the English king had held the right to call out all able-bodied freemen in times of emergency. However, usually, only a select few nearest to the conflict would be levied. All able-bodied Englishmen had the chance of being fyrd: the levy called up one man for every five 'hides' of land. They were farmers and tradesmen, among other occupations, who were only required to spend two months on military service during wartime, even during an invasion, before they were sent home. In this way they became used to war and trained by experience; there may also have been other training provided. Outside of wartime, they were only levied to build fortifications and repair bridges.

A final type of English military was the butsecarls. These appear to have been sailors who were equally adept at land and naval fighting, and they may have been paid for their services.

The Roman road between York and London was as straight as geography allowed and it was still in very good condition. For more than 800 years it had been maintained as the principal thoroughfare between the north and south. Had it been anything but, it is unlikely that Harold's troops could have achieved what they did next: they marched to York at the incredible pace of 20 to 25 miles (32 to 40km) per day, a feat rarely achieved by any pre-modern army, especially one undertaken mostly by infantry. While the huscarls may have travelled on horse, the fyrd were on foot.

Harold's English army arrived at Tadcaster on 24 September, the day that the Norwegians had moved to Stamford Bridge. Hearing that York had not received nor given hostages yet, the English king moved promptly into York. After a few short hours of rest, food and recovery, he marched his army to Stamford Bridge the next day.

The citizens of York had undoubtedly been surprised by the sudden appearance of their king. But theirs was not nearly the surprise of the Norwegians on the morning of 25 September. By his rapid pace of march Harold Godwinson had completely shocked his opponent. Of course, the Norwegian king's lack of caution at not posting guards or scouts certainly added to Harold's advantage at Stamford Bridge, but that lack of caution was based on experience. What experienced general – Harald had been taught to fight by

Scandinavian, Russian and Byzantine leaders and he had fought in wars throughout from Scandinavia to the Mediterranean – would have expected the English king to march over 200 miles (322km) in ten days? Harald reasonably thought the English army was far to the south of him.

In fact, Harald and Tostig had been so confident in their victories – so certain that they still had several days before any relief army might arrive from the south – that they had divided their army in Stamford Bridge, letting a large number of soldiers take advantage of the good weather to bathe in the water of the river or rest on the meadow that was on the opposite side of the bridge from the main army. 'They were all very cheerful', writes the author of *Morkinskinna*. The men enjoying themselves under the autumn sun had taken their weapons with them, but they'd left their shields and armour behind with the rest of the army.

It was probably those in the main army on the hill above the bridge, in an area known today as Battle Flats, who first caught sight of what appeared to be a large group of men approaching them. At first they thought these were the citizens of York bringing the promised hostages. But as the numbers of men grew, so too did the confusion of the Norwegians. According to Snorri Sturluson, Harald called Tostig to him, asking if he knew whether the approaching men were hostile or not. The earl was as befuddled as he. But soon enough, the men marching towards them had grown into an army, their weapons glistening in the sun. 'They looked like broken ice' is how the author of *Fagrskinna* puts it.

Harald and Tostig now realized that this was the army of the English king. They began to shout to their men in the water and on the meadow below, with some of the Norwegians even rushing down towards them. If their warnings were understood, they had come too late: the English quickly recognized the situation and didn't hesitate before rushing down upon the cut-off, poorly armed soldiers and slaughtering them.

Some, not many, of the Norwegian army on the other side of the river were able to cross the bridge and join their fellow soldiers. They were quickly followed by raging, charging English soldiers, who needed to be stopped if there was to be any chance for the main

The Shield-wall

By the eleventh century the chief defensive tactic used in England and Scandinavia was the shield-wall. In this formation the soldiers would overlap their shields with their spears, unsharpened ends anchored firmly in the ground, protruding out from behind them. It was, in essence, a field fortification designed for defence against almost any charge by infantry or cavalry, providing a protection for those inside until their opponents grew fatigued and ceased their attacks.

Shield-walls were generally straight and quite solid, capable of defending front, rear and flanks. But at times a very adept general might alter the formation to suit the terrain or counter greater numbers. This appears to be what Harald Hardrada did at Stamford Bridge, where the Norwegian Kings' Sagas assert that he ordered his soldiers in a 'long and thin formation … the wings bent back so that they came together … shield over shield overlapping on the top'.

A shield-wall could usually be broken only at the cost of many men. But in some cases, as at both Stamford Bridge and Hastings, those inside the shield wall themselves grew weary of fighting in such a manner and they would 'break out' from their positions of safety to try and defeat the opposing force with their own charges. At Hastings, William the Conqueror seems to have engaged in at least two 'feigned retreats' – an ancient tactic meant to cause those in a defensive formation, like a shield-wall, to believe they were retreating from the battlefield – luring some of the English troops to break and follow after them. As the retreat was only feigned, however, the attackers regrouped and turned back on the now very vulnerable English soldiers, riding them down.

The English shield-wall, from the Bayeux Tapestry. (*Musée de la Tapisserie de Bayeux*)

Norwegian army to outfit themselves in armour and organize their shield-wall. This led to one of the more heroic and – at least among the more contemporary English and Norman sources – more often recorded incidents of the battle. One Norwegian warrior across the bridge had been wearing his armour. Rather than retreat across the bridge with his companions, we are told, he stood in front of it and single-handedly defended it from those English soldiers trying to cross. Swinging his large battleaxe, he killed more than forty. William of Malmesbury records that he was called to surrender and that the English would welcome 'a man of such physical strength' with 'generous treatment'. He refused, taunting them, 'they were a poor lot if they could not deal with a single man'. The fighting stopped. No one would approach him, 'rendered more incautious by justified confidence', until one of the huscarls threw an iron spear at him and 'pierced him through'. An alternative story has him stabbed in the groin by a spear from a soldier on a boat under the bridge.

This brave defiance allowed Harald and Tostig to recover from their surprise and regroup their men. Tostig suggested that they may want to retreat to their ships, where they had more men and a means to escape should the battle turn against them. But Harald wanted none of that. The Norwegians held the high ground and could easily establish a defensive position. The English would become quite fatigued having to climb the hill to attack it. Even should they fail, 'the English will have an exceedingly difficult battle before we are killed', the *Fagrskinna* reports Harald saying. He then sent three riders 'on the fastest horses' to warn the men at his ships of the battle and to request their aid.

The Norwegian king ordered his troops into a shield-wall, positioning his household guards with Tostig and his most faithful troops inside the circle surrounding his standard, *Land-waster*. These experienced soldiers could move forward and strengthen those parts of the shield-wall that weakened. The few Norwegian archers that were with his army also remained inside the shield-wall.

Twenty English horsemen, 'all clad in mail armour', broke from their ranks and rode toward the Norwegian lines. One called out to Tostig, telling him that his brother wanted peace. Harold would give Tostig one-third of his kingdom, including Northumbria. But the exiled earl refused. If this had been offered before he was exiled, Tostig responded, 'then many men would still have their lives, but now do not. Then England would not be the worse country that it is now.'

The English horseman also had an offer for Harald Hardrada: 'seven feet of space or more length as he is taller than other men'. The English riders returned to their lines. Sensing that Tostig seemed to know the English spokesman, Harald asked: 'Who was that eloquent man?' 'That was King Harold Godwinson', Tostig answered.

If we trust the Norwegian Kings' Sagas, the Battle of Stamford Bridge saw the English making repeated cavalry charges against a shield-wall that was built because Harald knew 'that cavalry was accustomed to charge forward and quickly to ride back'. As a result, the Norwegian king ordered those standing in the front rank of the shield-wall that 'they should set their spear-shafts into the ground and place the points into the breasts of the cavalry soldiers, if they charge into us' and those standing behind them to 'set their spearheads against the breasts of their horses'. And so it happened: the English cavalry charged against the shield-wall, were stopped, then retreated, regrouped and charged again.

Did the English Fight as Cavalry?

The vision of the battle presented in the Norwegian Kings' Sagas has been a problem for some historians, who point out that the English army, up to the time of this battle, had not shown proficiency in cavalry charges. But of course this hardly means they were ignorant of the tactics involved. And the simple fact is that the Norwegian Kings' Sagas are our only source for information about the actions taken on the field. If we don't accept them as valid accounts of the battle, we simply have no idea what occurred at Stamford Bridge!

The Norwegian shield-wall withstood several of these cavalry charges. But soon it began to weaken, the English were simply too numerous to hold out against them for long. Harald Hardrada decided to change tactics. His shield-wall suddenly dissolved, as the Norwegian soldiers broke out of their formation to make their own charge against the English. Harald surely thought that he had a chance, by delivering an unexpected thrust at the English, of driving them from the battlefield and giving his troops victory –

just as Morkere had tried to do to him at Fulford Gate. After all, the Norwegian army may have been smaller in numbers, but they were mostly trained and experienced soldiers. And they were vicious, with the blood of Viking ancestors flowing through their veins. Surely, the fyrd, who filled the ranks of the English army, would flee as they saw these warriors charging at them.

But they didn't. 'There was a great slaughter among both armies', is how the Norwegian Kings' Sagas describe the next few minutes of combat. Harald Hardrada was particularly valiant in this charge, fighting without a shield or his long mail-shirt that he so prized that he had named it *Emma*. A poet would remember him later: 'Norway's king had nothing / To shield his breast in battle; / And yet his war-seasoned / Heart never wavered. / Norway's warriors were watching / The blood-dripping sword / Of their courageous leader / Cutting down his enemies.'

The Naming of Weapons

Such was the importance (and expense) of swords in Viking culture that they were often given names and passed down through the generations. In *Laxdæla Saga* a woman named Thuríd, wronged by her husband Geirmund, stole his boat and his sword, *Fótbítr* (Leg-biter). So much did he value the blade that he offered her whatever riches she wanted for its return. For the very same reason, she refused to give it back. As common as the naming of swords might've been, we have far less evidence of the naming of armour. Whatever else we can say about Harald Hardrada, he liked his armour!

The fighting spirit and bravery of the Norwegians was fierce. But it could not break the English resolve and ultimately their greater numbers prevailed. In the end, the charge did not gain the result the Norwegian king hoped; many of his soldiers were slain. Harald himself was killed, struck in his unarmoured throat by an arrow.

Tostig Godwinson did not charge with Harald and the other Norwegians. He may not have understood what Harald was doing, the command to charge given quickly with undoubtedly too little time to explain what was happening to a foreign ally who had not trained with these soldiers. With the death of Harald Hardrada, however, Tostig found himself in command of those who remained. He quickly called a retreat to their former position and tried to re-establish a shield-wall.

Once again, Harold Godwinson approached and offered peace to Tostig and all the remaining Norwegians, but the poet concludes: 'All King Harald's warriors / Preferred to die beside him, / Sharing their brave king's fate, / Rather than beg for mercy'. It took only minutes. Tostig was also shot in the face by an English arrow.

Within these last moments of battle the Norwegian reinforcements from the ships arrived at Stamford Bridge. These soldiers had run all the way from Ricall and were very fatigued by the time they reached the battlefield. Most were unarmoured and carried no shields, only their weapons. Nevertheless, they tried to fight. Their slaughter continued until after dark.

Non-saga sources contain none of this, except for the length of the battle and the high number of casualties on both sides. The English had won the victory, but it was costly. King Harold Godwinson had lost many men, although no sources record just how many. But the Norwegians had lost far more than the English, including their leaders, Harald and Tostig – the latter's face so mangled by his wound that he was identified by the wart between his shoulders. His brother commanded that he be taken back to York and buried in an unnamed church there. He then allowed the remnants of the defeated army, both those who remained at the ships and those captured at Stamford Bridge, to return to Norway. The army that had been brought on more than 300 ships now left on only 20.

The English army retired from the battlefield to York. The Norwegian invasion of England had come to an end.

But the Norman invasion, on the southern coast of England, had just begun.

TOUR TWO: TOSTIG'S JOURNEY

Though often forgotten, Tostig Godwinson is one of the most important figures in any history of 1066: not only was he a central player (if not architect) of the Norwegian invasion of England, but his actions also inadvertently aided in the success of the Norman Conquest by weakening Harold's ability to defend his lands.

Tostig's winding path around the North Sea in 1066 means that only the most diehard adventurers will seek to follow him from Bruges to Stamford Bridge. For those who do so, however, the journey passes through a number of remarkable sites. They are presented here not in a tour of localized stops but as a sequence of places to be visited.

Bruges

A comital fortress in Bruges, the *burg*, is first mentioned during the reign of the third count of Flanders, Arnulf I (r. 918–65). When it was built is not known and it may even have predated the establishment of the county of Flanders by Baldwin I in 863. Arnulf is recorded to have enlarged it and changed it to a square shape – although what its earlier shape had been is unknown. Arnulf also built the Church of Saint Donatian (later a cathedral) in an octagonal style with a Romanesque nave and enclosed the whole *burg* with a wooden stockade – it is likely that this was replacing an earlier earthen rampart.

By the time of Baldwin V all of this still existed, although Arnulf's wooden stockade had been replaced by a stone wall. Over the previous century Bruges had become a major trading centre which had greatly enriched the city and the count. So Baldwin would further enlarge the fortress to accommodate the needs and luxury he expected as a much wealthier lord.

It is in this castle that Baldwin V lived and undoubtedly received Godwin and his family on their numerous visits to the city; they probably stayed there as well, although several monasteries in and near Bruges could have hosted them. Saint Donatian's was also likely where Tostig and Judith were married, although by the mid-eleventh century the people of Bruges had built another church that they dedicated to Saint Walpurga, a favourite among wealthy women. This, too, could have been the site of the wedding.

Part of the city wall erected around Bruges in the tenth century. (*Kelly DeVries*)

Saint Donatian's was destroyed by French Revolutionary occupiers in 1799. Little more than a few of its stones can still be seen above ground. The shape of Baldwin's castle, which was not extended further after the counts moved their 'official' residence to Ghent in the twelfth century, can be envisioned in the shape of a square, still known as the *burg*, that extends from the old site of Saint Donatian.

In 1955, workers digging a large cellar beneath the Crown Plaza Brugge Hotel, which stands on the north-east side of the *burg*, uncovered the remains of the octagonal foundations of Saint Donatian's, along with a stretch of the eleventh-century stone wall and several staves of the tenth-century wooden rampart. These remnants of Tostig's time can be seen by asking permission at the front desk to visit the downstairs.

The foundations of the Saint Donatian Church, built in Bruges in 950 and destroyed in 1799. (*Kelly DeVries*)

Bruges is one of the best preserved and most beautiful medieval cities in Europe, with nearly every building facade a work of art. While still in the *burg* a visit to the Basilica of the Holy Blood is important. This small church was built between 1134 and 1157 as a chapel for the private worship of the count of Flanders, Thierry of Alsace. It was the perfect location to place the reliquary of the Holy Blood, brought back from the sack of Constantinople in 1204 by Flemish Count Baldwin IX's forces. (Baldwin himself would stay in Byzantium, elected the new Latin Emperor of Constantinople, until he disappeared following the defeat of the Crusader army to the Bulgars outside of Adrianople on 14 April 1205; legend holds that Tsar Kaloyan made his skull into a drinking cup.) The actual relic, the blood, cannot be seen, but is in a Byzantine rock crystal phial, sealed with red wax and gold thread and dated to the eleventh or twelfth century, placed within a gold cylinder closed at the ends by coronets, of Flemish make dated to 3 May 1388. Yearly, on the Day of Ascension (the Thursday before Easter), the Holy Blood is paraded through the streets of Bruges in one of the most visited processions in Belgium. Several other medieval art works can be found in the Basilica, which was altered in the fifteenth century and again in 1823.

Outside of the old centre are several other sites of medieval interest – gates and churches. The most beautiful of the latter is the *Onze-Lieve-Vrouwekerk* (Church of Our Lady) which dates from the thirteenth to the fifteenth centuries. The building is a most beautiful

The Halletoren was built in Bruges in 1240 (with the top level added in the fifteenth century). Its 366 steps lead to extraordinary vistas of the city and surrounding environs. (*Kelly DeVries*)

Gothic church, with impressive flying buttresses (built in the latter half of the thirteenth century) and a brick tower measuring 379ft (115.6m). Inside are the tombs of the Burgundian Duke Charles the Bold (r. 1422–77) and his daughter, Duchess Mary of Burgundy (r. 1477–82). Note especially the contemporary tomb paintings made during the original burials. There are several other medieval works of art in the church. But no doubt the most beautiful in Our Lady is Michelangelo's sculpture of the Madonna and Child made in 1504–06. It is simply one of Michelangelo's finest works of art, made by the sculptor when only in his twenties.

An interesting feature of Our Lady Church is a private balcony that can be accessed only by a bridge leading from the large mansion across an alley in between the two. This balcony allowed private worship for the family of Lodewijk van Gruuthuis (also known as Louis de Bruges). Lodewijk was a lesser noble in the court of Burgundian duke Philip the Good (r. 1419–67), but he was brilliant and quickly recognized for his potential administrative genius. As a young man he was trained for war – knighted at the battle of Gavere in 1453 – and won prizes in a number of tournaments; he also became a Knight of the Golden Fleece in 1461. But his real worth was as a chief councillor, first to Philip, then to his son, Charles the Bold, then to his daughter, Mary of Burgundy, and finally to her husband, Emperor Maximilian of Austria. When he died in 1492 at the age of 67, he was the wealthiest man in one of the wealthiest cities in Europe. Lodewijk was a patron of arts and his house is a monument of medieval urban architecture, begun in the thirteenth century but greatly improved in the mid-fifteenth century. It is filled with carvings and paintings of his newly-acquired heraldry, a large gunpowder artillery piece, called a mortar by a contemporary Burgundian chronicler. The *Gruuthuse Museum* (fee required) that occupies Lodewijk's house today is filled with historical artefacts from his century and later.

Any visit to Bruges must include the *Halletoren*, the belfry built in 1240 (rebuilt in 1280 after a fire destroyed much of it). This was a period of rivalry among the southern Low Countries cities, their wealth expended on public buildings, artistic works and book manuscripts. As their wealth was derived from the cloth industry that each were involved with, *halletorens* (cloth towers and buildings) were constructed. None were as magnificent as the one built in Bruges.

When completed – the top story was added between 1483 and 1487 – it measured 272ft (83m). A climb of 366 steps offers the most beautiful vistas, including the square below, where numerous tournaments were held in the fifteenth century. Don't worry if you've seen the film *In Bruges*: there is actually no way to fall from the tower!

Denmark
We don't know for certain where Tostig met with King Sweyn II Estridsson in Denmark, but odds are good that it was in Roskilde,

The Skuldelev 5 ship was excavated from the Roskilde fjord in 1962. (*Kelly DeVries*)

which had a royal residence. The wooden precursor to Roskilde Cathedral was destroyed when the Gothic building was built in the twelfth and thirteenth centuries. Sweyn, who was buried in the previous church, was reinterred in one of the pillars, its place marked by a modern plaque.

While in Roskilde, a visit to the *Vikingeskibsmuseet* (Viking Ship Museum) is a must. It holds the remains of five Viking ships that were scuttled to block the Skuldelev Channel of the Roskilde fjord around 1070. These were excavated in 1962 and underwent extensive restoration. Four of the ships are small, wide and low-hulled cargo vessels, but one is the largest extant Viking vessel (identified as Skuldelev 5-7 – it was initially mistaken to be three ships – or Skuldelev 6), measuring at 118ft (36m). Dendrochronology has confirmed that this ship was constructed from English wood.

The Danevirke earthen wall, stretching across a part of the Jutland peninsula, was begun c.500 but extended in the eighth and ninth centuries to protect Denmark from the Franks. (*Kelly DeVries*)

Given the date at which these ships were scuttled, it might have been Sweyn Estridsson who gave the order to do so; he died in 1076. The Museum also contains reconstructions of the excavated vessels. If the weather is good, a short journey into the fjord can also be booked.

A look at what the people, economics and culture of a medieval Danish town such as Roskilde would be like can be seen through a visit to the Archaeological Border Complex of Hedeby and the Danevirke on southern Jutland, just south of the Danish-German border. Founded in 770, the town of Hedeby barely survived an attack in 1050 by Harald Hardrada, who was then at war with Sweyn Estridsson, only to be completely destroyed by Slavs in 1066. The town was subsequently abandoned, its few survivors journeying across the fjord to Schleswig. Harald's was the most damaging of the two attacks, with Snorri Sturluson writing, 'Burnt in anger from end to end was Hedeby ... High rose the flames from the houses'. Anything able to be pillaged was, with most of the population being massacred.

After 1066 there was no further habitation, making it the perfect site for a series of archaeological excavations (1900–15, 1930–9 and 1959–present). What has been found has revolutionized all interpretations of Scandinavian life, especially as it stood in the eleventh century. It has dismissed the idea that Vikings existed only as primitive warriors who lived to brutally plunder foreign lands. Hedeby had a diverse and rich culture, supported by strong trade with all nearby lands. The town supported all the crafts and occupations of any other northern European town, including, evidently, competent surgery and dentistry. Its citizens had dietary ranges that rivalled anywhere else in Europe. The many finds can all be seen in the large and impressive *Wikinger Museum Haithabu* (Hedeby Viking Museum).

Hedeby was surrounded by large earthen fortifications that arced around the city, protecting it from assaults on land – unfortunately Harald's attack came from the sea. The remnants of these can still be seen, although Google Earth provides the best view of the whole. They connect to an inland earthen wall, the *Danevirke*. This fortification was built in stages, with the oldest sections dating to roughly AD 500 and the latest to the tenth century. The *Danevirke* is still 19 miles (30km) long today, with a height varying between 12ft and 20ft (3.6m and 6m); in the Middle Ages it was probably taller and surmounted by a wooden palisade. Several sections can be visited by car, but its entire length can be walked. It very certainly originated as a defensive structure, but for whom and against whom it was protecting is unknown. However, it would continue to be used for defensive purposes through the First World War.

Trondheim

Although there is some dispute, Harald Hardrada probably never got his seven feet of land in England. The Norwegian Kings' Sagas

The Nidaros Cathedral was built from the eleventh to the thirteenth century over the burial spot of King (Saint) Olaf in modern Trondheim. (*Kelly DeVries*)

say that his body was allowed to be taken back to Norway aboard one of the twenty ships that returned to his kingdom – other sources report that it was not returned until after William the Conqueror became king. Initially it was buried in Saint Mary's Church in Nidaros (modern Trondheim), but about a century later and for no recorded reason, it was moved to Helgeseter Priory in the same city. That monastery was demolished in the seventeenth century – although monks had not lived there for many decades by the time of its destruction – but Harald's body was not reinterred. Since 2006, there has been a concerted effort by Norwegian historical groups, especially in Trondheim, to have the site of the former priory, now covered over by a large road, excavated and Harald's body located. He would then be reburied in the nearby Nidaros Cathedral, to lie with his brother, Saint Olaf, next to whom he fought and was wounded at the Battle of Stiklestad on 30 July 1030, when Harald was only 15. There is a plaque commemorating the king near to where Harald is supposedly buried, but any citizen of Trondheim will be pleased to point out their own most favoured place for the site (although these are rarely the same).

Tostig may have visited Harald at Trondheim, although it is more likely that he visited the Norwegian king at Oslo, a city founded by Harald Hardrada to be his capital.

Oslo

After Harald Hardrada returned from Russia and Byzantium to Norway as king in 1046, he determined that a more southern capital was needed if the kingdom was to be closer to the rich trade offered by the rest of Europe. In 1048 he chose a small village at the end of a fjord with a well-protected harbour, Oslo. Although he would keep a residence in Trondheim, under Harald's influence Oslo grew in population and importance, which continued after Harald's death at Stamford Bridge. In 1070 the city became a bishopric and in 1300 it became the chief city of Norway.

Oslo is a beautiful city that offers much to the visitor, although not a lot remains from the Middle Ages – almost all of which was entirely built in wood, timber not being scarce in Scandinavia as it was elsewhere. Examples of these houses can be seen, though, in the open-air *Norsk folkemuseet* (Norwegian Museum of Culture) located

The Gol Stave Church, built in the twelfth and thirteenth centuries is one of the finest examples of a Norwegian wooden church. Faced with demolition it was moved to Oslo in 1880. (*Kelly DeVries*)

on Bygdøy peninsula, a short water-taxi trip from Oslo's centre. Among the many premodern structures brought to the museum from throughout Norway is one of the few remaining Stave Churches from the Middle Ages, the Gol Stave Church. Built between 1157 and 1216, the church was moved to the museum in 1884–5, fortunately preserving it from the town's plan of demolishing it and replacing it with a stone church. The exquisite carvings on the wooden beams and lintels are worth the visit alone (fee required).

Within walking distance from the *folkemuseet* is the *Vikingskipshuset* (Viking Ship Museum) which contains three Viking ships, including

The well-preserved ninth-century Gokstad ship was excavated from a burial mound in 1880. It is the longest Viking ship in Norway. (*Kelly DeVries*)

the two best-preserved ships still in existence (fee required). The Oseberg and Gokstad ships were excavated from ground burials, the cold earth preserving the entire ships. The Oseberg ship is also the oldest extant Viking vessel, dating to c.800 – it was buried in 834. It is built entirely of oak and measures 70.8ft (21.58m) in length and 16.7ft (5.1m) in width; its mast of 30–33ft (9–10m), a very rare survival, was buried within the ship, together with the best-preserved and beautifully-carved early medieval wooden carts, as well as other grave goods. Of great interest is that the ship contained the bodies of two women placed under a wooden tent. Dressed in the most luxurious of woollen and silk cloth, one is suggested to have been an elite woman, perhaps the wife of a Viking chieftain; the second, far less well dressed, was likely a servant or slave who chose or was forced to be buried with her mistress. The Gokstad ship is longer, at 78.1ft (23.8m), but the same width, 16.7ft (5.1m), as the Oseberg ship. Its mast is missing, but it has its entire side-post rudder still fastened to the hull. Dendrochronology has dated the wood used to build this ship to 890, meaning that, before it was interred, it was probably used to raid the coasts of England, Ireland and/or Europe. That it was a warship is confirmed by its dead occupant, a well-built man in his 40s or 50s around 6ft (181–183cm) tall. Other grave goods included three small boats, a wooden tent, riding equipment and a sledge, another anomalous artefact. Unfortunately, anything of value that was buried with this Viking, including his armour and weapons, appears to have been plundered before the ship was found in 1880. The third ship, the Tune, which dates to c.900, was also excavated from a burial mound, but is only a fragment of 61ft (18.7m) in length and 14ft (4.2m) in width. Also impressive, it pales in comparison to the Oseberg and Gokstad vessels.

Searching for medieval history, no trip to Oslo would be complete without visiting the *Kulturhistorisk museet* (Museum of Cultural History). Often missed by tourists, doubtlessly due to its similar name to the open-air museum or the fact that it is in the grounds of the University of Oslo, this museum holds an endless number of medieval artefacts from the Viking age and later (perhaps only rivalled in their number and quality by the National Museum of Denmark in Copenhagen). Viking-era caches and runestones are in abundance, as well as large numbers of arms and armour. There are swords, axeheads, spearheads and arrowheads to satisfy anyone, but not to be missed is one of the earliest and most complete mail armour, identical to those seen on the Bayeux Tapestry. Nor should the non-military medieval artefacts be missed. It's always fun to see that well into the late Middle Ages, Scandinavians wore both a cross and a Thor's hammer around their necks – one can never be too certain when it comes to the afterlife!

Isle of Wight

Situated as it is between the English Channel and the Solent, close to several historically significant ports on the mainland (Southampton and Portsmouth loom large), the Isle of Wight has long been a target for those seeking a foothold in England. At the end of the tenth century this meant Vikings, who began using it as a base for raids across the southern coasts of the island. By the middle of the next century, it wasn't necessarily Vikings who were raiding the island: in 1052 Earl Godwin and his sons used it as a rallying point in their quest to return from exile.

Of the few medieval remnants that survive today, the location most worth a visit is Carisbrooke Castle, which sits on a hill above Newport. The castle's site appears to have been occupied even before the Romans came to the area and it was an important location in the Early English period. When the Vikings began their raids, a defensive wall was built around the hill. After the Conquest, the Normans built a motte-and-bailey castle on the site, which was later built in stone and enlarged. Not surprisingly, it was the site of additional fortifications with the looming threat of the Spanish Armada during the reign of Queen Elizabeth I.

Dunfermline

Between its departure from Norway and its anchoring at Ricall – or in the case of Tostig of the Isle of Wight and Ricall – the path of the invading fleet is marked only with generic place- and waterway-names. The only two exceptions are Dunfermline and Scarborough.

Dunfermline is where Harald met with King Malcolm III of Scotland. The town may have been purpose-built as a new royal centre by Malcolm sometime around 1050 – it is not mentioned previously – with later records reporting that he married his second wife, Margaret (canonized in 1250) in the city between 1068 and 1070. Nothing still exists from the eleventh century, although much of the Dunfermline Abbey church founded in 1128 remains. (It was sacked during the Reformation in 1560 and repurposed as a Protestant Church afterwards, so no medieval decorations are extant.)

Scarborough

The headland above Scarborough shows archaeological signs of occupation during the Stone and Iron Ages, as well as being the location of a Roman signal station during the fourth century – one of many such stations that were built along the coasts of Britannia. According to tradition, the medieval town surrounding the bay below the headland was founded around AD 966 by a Viking raider-

Overlooking the city of Scarborough is a massive twelfth-century castle. It is from this bluff that Harald Hardrada's troops sent fiery logs onto the townspeople below. (*Kelly DeVries*)

turned-settler named Thorgils Skarthi. The place was named Skarthaborg and it grew slowly and steadily. Archaeologists have verified the significant amount of fire destruction caused by the attack of Harald Hardrada in 1066, by which time it was a thriving village of many houses that largely prospered from fishing and smuggling. The town did rebuild, however, and once again found prosperity, especially after the headland was surrounded with a large wall and a royal castle built by Henry II between 1155 and 1168. Probably because of its isolation, it became a favourite residence for Henry's son, John; later it would also become the stage for the capture of Piers Gaveston, King Edward II's favourite (and perhaps his lover), who was chased to this castle before being executed. As a royal castle, it was captured by Oliver Cromwell in the English Civil War. He pulled down part of its walls, which has left the strange existence of half a castle, as if it were a cake with half cut away from it. Other ruined buildings surround the castle, including the queen's house, with a less than luxurious but obvious toilet. Scarborough Castle is always a great place to visit, and a stroll around the wall provides a great walk, with the ruins of the Roman Signal Station well preserved at its very tip.

Most of the rest of Scarborough has transformed into a family resort, with its bay of nice sand and North Sea swimming, that children will love – even as adults will always, even in summer, find it a bit chilly.

Ricall

Trying to determine exactly where Harald and Tostig anchored their ships on the Ouse River is practically impossible. Almost all of the sources, both saga and non-saga narratives, provide the name of Harald and Tostig's chief anchorage spot as Ricall, but determining the exact location they had in mind is practically impossible. The earlier sources all claim that there was little habitation at the site and sufficient riverbank to anchor 300 ships, but today the town of Ricall is a modern bedroom community of some 4,000 people serving the larger nearby cities of York and Leeds – with no clear indication how the banks of the Ouse here ever could have supported Harald and Tostig's large fleet. It may be that changes to the course of the river over the past millennium – especially diversions for the Ricall Coal Mine which operated from 1983 to 2004, as well as for the numerous agricultural projects that have made use of the river – have erased the information we would need from the landscape.

Visitors to Ricall should note the nearby late Anglo-Saxon church, Saint Mary's, though it is not mentioned in any of the sources reporting the Norwegian fleet being anchored here.

Fulford Gate

Travelling north from Ricall, a modern road sign along the A19 indicates that one has reached Fulford Gate – a suburb 2 miles (3km) south of the city of York. The Battle of Fulford Gate was found *somewhere* around here. As with so many pre-modern battles, its exact site has not been positively identified. Any artefacts that might have been found in the fields by early amateur archaeologists are either lost or lacking the necessary provenance. As a result, several competing sites have been suggested. Local historical and archaeological groups have even gone to court to stop development of where they thought the battle was fought: but on each occasion

Where the Battle of Fulford Gate was fought is unknown, with only street signs to indicate the modern suburb of York.

they have been unable to satisfy judges or juries that their location of the battlefield should be preserved. This is largely because the three elements that we have about the battlefield from the original sources – the Roman road, the Ouse river and the large swampland – have all changed or disappeared completely over the past 1,000 years. The road has been enlarged and raised, the river's size and course has been altered over the years by irrigation and other water-using projects and the swamp has been drained and built upon. Until such time that a professional archaeological study can be made of the land and significant finds are located, the battlefield of Fulford Gate must be considered lost.

York
Neither the Norwegian nor the English armies spent much time in York. Harald negotiated the surrender of the city outside its walls and arranged that hostages would be exchanged at Stamford Bridge. It is not known why he did not enter the city at the time or

Among the medieval walls that stretch around York is this tower built either in the mid-seventh or mid-ninth centuries and commonly, although perhaps erroneously, known as the Anglian Tower today. (*Kelly DeVries*)

why the people of York agreed to surrender to him without making the Norwegian king besiege it. We know the Romans built strong walls around the city, with parts still extant, including an amazing Roman multiangular tower outside of the ruins of Saint Mary's monastery – one of the most powerful monasteries in northern England, which would, however, not be founded until after the Norwegian and Norman conquests of 1066. At times following the Romans' abandonment of the city in the early fifth century, the population tried to maintain the Roman walls and even build new towers, as can be seen in the Anglian Tower, built in the south-

The cathedral of York, dedicated to Saint Peter, was built in the thirteenth–fifteenth centuries. (*Kelly DeVries*)

west area of the later medieval walls. This rather interesting tower was built sometime in the reign of King Edwin II of Northumbria (r. 616–32) to cover a breach in the Roman walls. By the eleventh century the Roman walls had proved unable to contain the growing population of the city and both the Anglian and Viking communities had chosen to build homes outside the walls – with the walls and other Roman monuments raided for building materials.

A visitor to York today will surely be able to visit the Roman and Anglian towers, as well as several churches that predate the conquest. A museum commemorating the Viking settlement (The Jorvik Viking Centre) is especially worth a visit. This excellent experiential museum shows both the archaeological excavations that continue to take place as well as a reconstruction of the Viking

The second motte-and-bailey castle built in York by William the Conqueror was crowned by a stone castle in the thirteenth century. Its name ironically comes from the Baron Roger Clifford, whose executed body was dangled from its walls following the defeat of a baronial rebellion against the king at the Battle of Boroughbridge in 1322. (*Kelly DeVries*)

village of c.AD 1000. (Any young person will be thrilled to hear that the conservators of the Museum have recreated the sights, sounds and especially smells of the village. Be prepared to have all the outhouses pointed out when you pass by them!)

There are many later medieval sites to visit in York: a walk around the walls; visiting the Minster (especially taking a trip into the crypt that houses the site where Constantine declared himself emperor of the Roman Empire in AD 305), plus two of the earliest Anglo-Norman motte-and-bailey castles, Baile Hill and Clifford's Tower, although the stone castle was not built on the latter until the middle of the thirteenth century. (It gets its name from having Lord Clifford's corpse dangled off the walls after he was executed by Edward II for opposing him in a rebellion that met its end at the nearby town of Boroughbridge in 1323.) Clifford's Tower was also the site of one of the most brutal Jewish pogroms undertaken in England during the Middle Ages, when in 1190 more than 200 Jews barricaded themselves in the castle against an anti-Semitic mob who wanted to attack them. Before the uprising could be calmed, more than 150 had jumped to their death from the walls of the castle.

Stamford Bridge

The exact location where the Battle of Stamford Bridge was fought is not known today. Original sources, even the Norwegian Kings' Sagas, are vague on the topography of the battlefield, indicating only the prominence of the Derwent River, a tributary of the Ouse River, running through the battlefield with a narrow wooden bridge crossing over it. On the western bank of the river, the side approached by Harold Godwinson's army on the morning of 25 September, there was a wide, slightly sloped meadow. On the eastern bank of the river, where Harald Hardrada perhaps placed his camp, there was higher ground, the slope of which rose more sharply from the riverbank. On this Harald formed his shield-wall, with the battle fought around and below it.

Today, the river is a narrow, sluggish stream, but its size and course have undoubtedly changed since 1066. The original bridge, too, has disappeared. Now the visitor to the town crosses the river

Precisely where the Battle of Stamford Bridge was fought is unknown, although it was likely near to where this modern bridge crosses the Derwent River.

over a wide, two-lane stone bridge. This new crossing is possibly placed over the site of the older structure, but as no archaeological remains of the earlier bridge have been found, even this cannot be concluded for certain.

Without knowing the course of the river or the location of the medieval bridge in 1066, it is almost impossible to know where the first phase of the battle was fought. The second phase of the battle is easier to locate, but only if the name Battle Flats can be trusted, assigned as it is to an area of higher ground located to the south-east of the present town's centre. This area, about 50ft (15m) above the Derwent River, is today a large sloping plain. Farmed now, it is difficult to know if Battle Flats was always as large or sloping as it is today. Could it also have accommodated as many as the 15,000 to 18,000 soldiers who would have used it as a battlefield?

Battle Flats is at least where tradition says that the main part of the battle took place. It is also a tradition that during the eighteenth century skeletons and weapons were found on Battle Flats, though nothing of these rumoured finds survives today. Nor has extensive metal-detection work found anything further.

Chapter 4

WILLIAM'S ROAD
TO HASTINGS

With the wind at last in his favour, William set sail for England on the night of 27 September 1066, at the head of his fleet of perhaps 1,000 ships. We don't know his exact route across the English Channel, though it seems safe to assume that he made the crossing more or less direct from the mouth of the Somme. This was, after all, the point of waiting for a southerly wind: it minimized manoeuvres, which was of utmost importance given the surely simple nature of many of the ships he had conscripted. Even following a straight

Saxon Shore Forts

To protect the vulnerable southern coast of Britain from raiders, the Romans constructed a number of large fortresses between the Isle of Wight and Norfolk during the third century AD. These were characterized by high and thick walls, exceeding 23ft (7m) in height and on average 14ft (4.3m) in width and covering a large area, between 3.7 and 10 acres (1.5 and 4 hectares). Most were of rectangular shape, similar to traditional Roman fortresses, and almost all were supported by large D- or U-shaped towers designed to support Roman artillery. Each fort had two large main gates on opposite sides, with two smaller gates on the remaining two sides. Eleven of these fortifications still exist, with several still in excellent condition. The *Notitia Dignitatum* (*List of Offices*), written c.390–420, records the names of nine of these, naming them the 'Saxon Shore' forts.

Probable routes of Harold and William to the south coast of England in 1066. (*Michael Livingston*)

course with the wind at their backs, however, fear of both storm and separation would have been very much on the minds of the men during the night.

Not that arrival on English shores would mean security. Despite the high likelihood of information crossing the Channel in the form of spies or merchant informants, the Normans cannot have been

The Normans land at Pevensey, from the Bayeux Tapestry. (*Musée de la Tapisserie de Bayeux*)

completely certain what resistance would meet them. Something of the danger they faced is clear from a story that William of Poitiers tells about two ships that lost touch with the fleet and instead came ashore near the town of Romney: the townspeople slaughtered these unfortunate Normans.

For the rest of the fleet, the morning of 28 September brought them following a rising tide into a landing at Pevensey, a small village nestled around the Saxon Shore fort that the Romans had called Anderitum. The site is now called Pevensey Castle and is the subject of the first part of Tour Three.

The landscape around Pevensey Castle today could hardly be more different from the one that William would have encountered in 1066. Understanding this difference, in fact, is a starting point toward understanding why William would choose this as a landing spot in the first place – which, absent any other evidence, we must assume it was.

Pevensey Castle today sits at the eastern end of a hill more than a mile from the shingled beaches of Pevensey Bay, overlooking the broad green swath of the Pevensey Levels National Nature Reserve, through which runs the A259 as it makes its way to Bexhill and, further on, Hastings. In 1066, however, the Roman fort at which

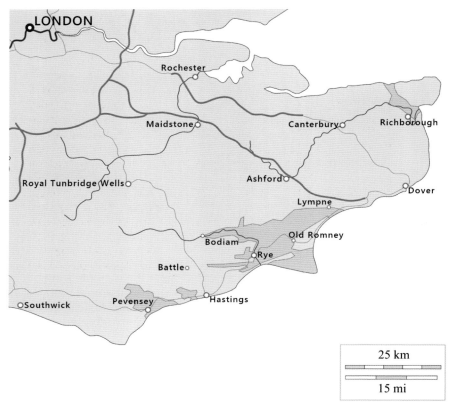

Major cities and roads of south-east England, showing approximate difference of coastline in 1066: areas shaded in light blue were then underwater. (*Michael Livingston*)

William arrived sat upon a peninsula, with the open sea at its feet and a sweeping tidal marsh stretching around and behind it. Today, the town of Normans Bay – on ground that was then under the sea – takes its name from this lost body of water and the fleet that so famously came here almost a thousand years ago. Bexhill, almost seven miles from Pevensey Castle, marked the other side of the mouth of the bay.

Between Bexhill and Hastings there was a now-vanished harbour at Bulverhythe that reached up into the Combe Valley, and Hastings itself would have had an arm of the sea stretching inland into the Priory Valley, west of the promontory on which Hastings Castle now stands.

Further east, the great headland of Dungeness today shelters a broad, flat landscape that was formerly the Romney Marsh and other wetlands. In 1066 this was a hundred-square-mile lagoon at the mouth of the River Rother, which at that time was tidal up its course as far as Bodiam and emptied into the Channel between Romney and Lydd. Several ports dotted the shores of this lagoon: Old Romney, Old Winchelsea, Lydd and Rye. The presence of this body of water, combined with those already mentioned, would have made Hastings a large peninsula, with its neck near to the very spot upon which William and Harold would fight for the throne of England.

There are many reasons that this south English landscape has changed so dramatically, but the most obvious of them is the waves

It was the movement of shingle beaches like this one, on the shores of Pevensey Bay, that helped reshape the coasts of England. (*Michael Livingston*)

of the sea: the relentless punishment of the ocean naturally makes any shoreline an ever-changing landscape. Yet the coast here is even more volatile still, changing dramatically over the centuries. The sharp currents through the English Channel would do damage enough on their own, but the fact that they can draw storms in from the North Atlantic makes matters exponentially worse. Without artificial stabilization and replenishment efforts, the popular beaches of today's southern shore might well disappear with the next major gale.

In fact, weather events along the Channel, could do more than just sweep away a beach; some were so powerful that they permanently altered coastlines. On 1 October 1250, an enormous storm rushed through the English Channel, shifting so much earth and rock that some bays and marshes and harbours were cut off from the sea. Another, on 4 February 1287, left Old Romney and Old Winchelsea without ports. Attempts to re-establish these towns back along the reconfigured tidal lines brought New Romney and Winchelsea Beach into existence over the years. As we will see later, the storm of 1287 took away part of Hastings Castle. And at the end of it all, Pevensey Castle no longer stood upon the sea. That one of these massive storms struck very nearly on the exact anniversary of William's crossing shows how right the Normans would have been to wait for good weather in 1066!

Godwin at Pevensey

According to the *Anglo-Saxon Chronicle* (E), just 14 years before William arrived there, Harold's father Godwin came to Pevensey at the head of a fleet, returning in force from his Flemish exile (see Chapter 1). He augmented his existing fleet with a number of ships that he stole from the port.

When we come to Pevensey, then, we must see it through the eyes of William in 1066: a Roman fortress beside a prosperous town, overlooking an enormous tidal bay that provided ample room for his fleet to anchor and come ashore, lifted in by the incoming tide.

That William would have known about this harbour – and in all likelihood the full extent of the English coastline and defences in this area – shouldn't surprise us in the slightest. The invasion had been in the planning for months and gathering information was integral to that effort. In that regard, this particular stretch of the English coastline would have been especially well-reconnoitred by the Normans: King Cnut had granted ownership of the manor of Rameslie (near present-day Rye) to the powerful Fécamp Abbey in Normandy and subsequent grants had given that abbey a swath of lands stretching to Hastings. Edward the Confessor had similarly granted to Fécamp the church at Steyning, 30 miles (50km) west of Pevensey, beginning in 1047.

Their local awareness of the landscape meant that as soon as the duke had made his intentions known regarding the crown of England, Fécamp's clergymen would have been a superb source of planning information. They were certainly no friends of Harold and his family, after all: just five years after Edward the Confessor had granted them Steyning, Earl Godwin had seized it for himself. So they had every reason to provide any and all knowledge that they would have had. Nor did they constrain themselves to information alone. Among the oaths taken by William before he left Normandy was his intention to return Steyning to the Norman abbey. The good monks of Fécamp, in return, gave him a ship for his invasion fleet.

William's first victory, like the D-Day landings of the Allies in Normandy on 6 June 1944, was simply getting ashore after crossing the Channel. By all accounts he did so unopposed. If there was a garrison at Pevensey, it abandoned its post almost at once: it cannot have been many men and the army coming ashore numbered in the thousands. The Norman ships would have filled the harbour and then some: allowing 30ft (10m) of space for each ship (enough to allow unloading of a vessel and prevent it from damaging other vessels nearby) means William needed a landing shore some 6 miles (10km) in length. They would surely have filled every available harbourage and beach, with some perhaps mooring as far along the shoreline as Hastings, though as many as possible would be coming directly ashore at Pevensey. After all, the Roman fortress that had been abandoned to the Normans there would have been integral to William's plans: seizing it gave him a pre-existing fortification for his forces to utilize as they established their beachhead. How useful it would have been and how William secured it, can still be seen on a tour of the site today.

TOUR THREE: PEVENSEY CASTLE AND SURROUNDS

Pevensey Castle
Castle Road, Pevensey BN24, UK
(lat. 50.820, long. 0.335)

Directions: Take the B2190 off the roundabout between the A27 and A259. A large car park provides ample off-street parking in an associated ticket-controlled lot on the east side of the castle.

1 *The East Roman Gate*
Approaching the archway of the East Roman Gate, located where the B2191 diverts around the castle, provides a clear image of what William found when he made a similar approach from the shoreline in 1066. The outer walls of the fortress are of Roman construction: 12ft (3.6m) thick and in places standing close to their original height at nearly 30ft (9m). That so much of this structure survives today, some seventeen centuries after it was built, is a testament to Roman engineering practices, which began with the digging of a ditch 15ft (4.6m) deep.

The East Gate of Pevensey Castle's Roman walls today. (*Michael Livingston*)

The excavated earth was used to raise and level the ground inside the fort. Down in the ditch, oak piles were driven even further into the earth, then sealed in with packed clay and flint around timber framing. After this foundation was cemented in place, the walls were built up in layers of stone. At their completion, the core of the Roman walls would have been faced with well-cut stones, but when the fort fell into disuse these provided tempting targets and were taken to be reused in other buildings. What is mostly visible today, then, is the raw, rubble infill of the Roman construction, with its telltale horizontal coursing of larger stones packed over smaller ones.

2 *Outer Bailey*

Passing through the East Gate, visitors enter the open expanse of what is now the Outer Bailey of Pevensey Castle – a post-Conquest construction whose moat and stone walls dominate the south-eastern corner of the site. There is an entrance fee to tour these later buildings (detailed below); visiting the rest of the site, however, is free.

To imagine the site as it was in Roman times – and at the time of William's arrival – one must erase the later constructions from the mind and focus primarily on the run of the outer walls, which enclosed a 10-acre (0.04km^2) site. While most Roman fortifications were square or rectangular, the shape of the peninsular promontory on which Pevensey was constructed pushed its engineers to follow a more oval shape, with the traditional corner towers moved closer to its ends to protect the approaches from the harbour and the road to the mainland, respectively. Portions of the northern and southern walls of the Roman fortification have today collapsed, but in William's day the northern ones and likely the southern ones, too, were still standing and in good order.

3 *West Gate*

Whether there were interior buildings when William arrived is unknown, but it appears that the only part of the Roman wall that was not then whole and defensible was the West Gate, which had been so robbed of stone – probably by locals in order to recycle these materials for their own projects – that William's first order after scouts were sent out was to construct a defensive barrier across the front of this gap with all speed.

Pevensey Castle's West Gate. The visible remains of the ditch dug by the Normans to defend this opening in the Roman walls is in the lower right. (*Michael Livingston*)

Stepping just outside the West Gate today, one can see the remains of this Norman ditch work on the southern side of the path, curving away from the street and around to the walls in the direction of the sea. As night fell on 28 September 1066 – the invaders' first day on English soil – the ditch would have been much deeper, with the excavated dirt flung up onto the eastern (inner) bank to further impede any assault from the mainland. Atop this the Normans might have put a wooden palisade.

Some have suggested that William did more than this, that he also erected an initial, 'prefabricated' castle on the site. This is extremely unlikely. He did not have the time to accomplish this, even if he had pre-built castle sections (which there is no record of existing) that he somehow transported (which there is no evidence of happening). What was prefabricated was what he found already on the shoreline: a ready-made fortification that was very efficiently made defensible. As he took his first sleep in England, William had his foothold. His next move would depend on the word from his scouts.

4 *St Mary's Church*

Visitors to Pevensey Castle are urged to make the short, 500ft (152m) walk east to St Mary's Church, Westham, which was one of the first churches built by the Normans after the Conquest, around the year 1080. The south wall of the church and its south transept – now remodelled into Priesthawes Chapel – retain their Norman walls, which are clearly identifiable by the rounded arches of their windows. The pillars and north wall date to the fourteenth century, while the tower dates to the fifteenth. The font likely dates to this period as well.

Parish Church of St Mary, perhaps the first Norman church in England. (*Kelly DeVries*)

5 *The Inner Bailey*

Returning to Pevensey Castle, visitors can pay a nominal fee to enter the later constructions of the Inner Bailey, which is well worth the time while here.

An initial inner bailey was built by the Normans in the twelfth century. It was larger than the stone structure now seen: its original size is indicated by the remains of a ditch that runs north-south across the site, dividing it in two. This ditch, now much filled-in, would have had a wooden palisade along its inside-edge, creating the first inner bailey in the eastern part of the grounds.

This initial layout was altered in the middle of the thirteenth century, when the Inner Bailey was reduced in size to the stone

The open field of what is today the Outer Bailey, looking south towards the walls of the Inner Bailey. The shallow ditch that stretches directly across this field are the remains of the post-Conquest ditch that initially split the Roman fort into an Outer Bailey to the right and an Inner Bailey to the left. (*Michael Livingston*)

A look across the Inner Bailey towards the ruins of the castle's later keep, with the foundations of a church in the right foreground. (*Michael Livingston*)

layout still present, now surrounded by a ditch that would have been far deeper and wider than it is today.

The Gatehouse, through which visitors enter the Inner Bailey, was constructed around 1200. It may have been an initial stage in converting the wooden structures to stone. The original defensive ditch was some 60ft (18m) wide, crossed by a wooden bridge, but by 1405 this was reduced to the stone causeway and wooden drawbridge now on site. Some 50 years after the Gatehouse was constructed, the curtain walls and the towers to the east and north were built. For unknown reasons, the towers to the west and south were still incomplete in 1317. They may never have been finished.

An interesting feature of Pevensey Castle is how its life continued into the twentieth century. In 1588 Tudor gun emplacements were installed on the south side of the Outer Bailey and the castle was refitted during the Second World War with pillboxes for machine guns and barracks for a garrison that found its billet here. Some of these military barracks were placed in the west and south towers.

Entering the Inner Bailey proper, two massive stone bases will be in view opposite the Gatehouse. These are the foundations of two of the towers of the Keep, which would have been the grand centre of the castle during the Middle Ages, filled with the living spaces of the lord in residence. Unfortunately, subsequent centuries saw this structure fall into such complete ruin that there is no way now to know its original design or layout.

Between the Gatehouse and the Keep, in the middle of the Inner Bailey, are the foundations of a small medieval church. When it was in use relative to the staging of the rest of the castle is as yet unknown. A stack of trebuchet stones stands in the grass nearby; these were found in the castle's moat and likely date to a siege of the castle in 1264.

Hastings would be the name that would be remembered in history, but Pevensey's pride of place as the Conquest's initial arrival point was what William remembered. In 1067, William left England to return to Normandy for the first time after he'd won his crown. For symbolic reasons he chose to embark from Pevensey. It was a moment of triumph and he used it to distribute conquered lands to his allies – including, very likely, Pevensey itself, which was given to Count Robert of Mortain, his half-brother. The castle would continue to play a role in English and Norman politics until it fell largely into disuse after the fourteenth century.

To Hastings

On 29 September 1066, his second day on English soil, William made the decision to move across the bay, from Pevensey to Hastings.

There are several reasons he may have done so. At this point, ashore in England, he would have been rapidly gaining any and all information he could get regarding the condition and whereabouts of Harold's forces. If he didn't have it beforehand, he would now have the news about the invasion of Hardrada and Tostig far to the north. It's even possible that he would have heard early whispers of Harold's extraordinary victory over them at Stamford Bridge, which was only three days past. Regardless, what he would know for certain was that Harold and his army were gone. For the moment, he had the southern coast to himself.

One possibility, then, is that William recognized that he had the opportunity in Harold's absence to establish a larger beachhead for his invasion and the Hastings peninsula better suited this intention than the far smaller one at Pevensey. He also might have recognized that a march toward London could be made easier if he departed from Hastings: major Roman roads – generally a preferred method of travel – ran from Hastings north to London. Depending on the route he took, along almost the entirety of this march he could even be within reach of the sea, which would give him both an escape route and a means of resupply or reinforcement. By contrast, from Pevensey the Roman roads ran across the English heartland far from the sea.

The enormous coastal changes along the Channel make it hard to know for certain what Hastings looked like in 1066. There was a mint here prior to the Conquest, which indicates a substantial settlement that was almost assuredly fortified. The early place-name 'Haestingaceastra', which appears in a 1050 entry of the *Anglo-Saxon Chronicle*, similarly indicates fortifications. Since no remains of such a settlement have been positively identified, we cannot be certain where it was located. The assumption that it would have been near to a harbourage provides us with several possible sites. From east to west, following the A259, the leading candidates (as we have already noted) are near Bulverhythe, between Bexhill and Hastings or on either side of the Priory Valley, to the east of which looms the promontory where Hastings Castle stands today. A best guess would put the fortification itself just east of Bulverhythe, in an area now under the earth, under pavements or – most likely – under the waves. Such was the size of the Norman fleet, however, that their 700–1,000 ships likely filled this entire stretch of ports during their initial disembarkation.

When William arrived – wherever he arrived – he once more rehabilitated the fortifications that he found on site. This was, as we will see, a hallmark of his campaign: taking advantage of existing

Hastings being fortified, from the Bayeux Tapestry. (*Musée de la Tapisserie de Bayeux*)

defensive works. As at Pevensey, the Normans were almost assuredly aided by information from the monks of Fécamp Abbey, who held much of the lands in the area.

As part of his army laboured to secure his new camp, William had his riders scouting the roads and villages of the Hastings peninsula to gather the most up-to-date information about the roads and by-ways and points of expected resistance. Behind them, foraging parties made their way into villages, acquiring foodstuffs for the army.

Much of the Hastings peninsula was covered in ridges and valleys whose deep woods gave the region the name it still has today: the Weald. The main Roman road out of Hastings ran over the ridge of the peninsula down to Sedlescombe and then north to a bridge over the River Rother at Bodiam. From there roads ran north to Rochester or east to Canterbury. In addition to these more substantial roads, there were tracks large and small cutting between villages. In Roman times, the Weald was heavily used for the production of iron – Beauport, on the northern edge of Hastings, may have had the third-largest iron works in the Empire – and because of this many of the smaller roads would have been useful for the passing of substantial armies even into William's time. The duke needed the most complete picture possible of these avenues of movement. Meanwhile, he needed to do all he could to gather supplies to be ready for the possibility that he would be in it for the long haul.

William didn't know the status of the English navy, but he knew the sea was a threat even without them: the coastline was often subject to raiders; only months earlier, as we have seen, Tostig had raided it himself. So, while Norman riders reconnoitred the roads and tracks, likely organizing scouting positions to warn him of attacks from the north, William of Poitiers informs us that William arranged many of his ships into a naval blockade of his beachhead.

In sum, he had quickly and efficiently established a very large base of operations. He was as secure as he could be at this point. No matter his confidence, he had to be stunned by his good fortune so far. Harald Hardrada and Tostig had inadvertently given him all the space he needed. But they might have felt the same on their arrival: the threat of William's invasion in the south had opened the north to them – only to have Harold manage a seemingly impossible march that surprised and destroyed them. So as good as William's luck had been, as well prepared as he tried to be, his biggest unknown was Harold.

The English king was still far to the north, only days from his extraordinary victory over Harald and Tostig at Stamford Bridge. But whatever the speed with which news of that battle reached the south coast of England, William would have to assume that news of his arrival there would have reached the north even faster. English alert systems meant that Harold would know he had arrived. The only question was how the king would respond.

One possibility would be that Harold would march south to meet him with all possible speed. Certainly Harold would not want to appear to have abandoned his own lands and people to the enemy. That could only result in the weakening of his authority. On the other hand, no matter the extent of his victory at Stamford Bridge, his forced march north and the intense fighting he had faced once there meant that his army was lessened. Worse, Harold would not have been ignorant that with winter approaching many of his men would have been anxious to return to their homes and farms, to ensure that crops were harvested and livestock secured for the cold months. These men had answered Harold's call to go north; that duty fulfilled, many of them might well slip away going south. A second strategy, then, would be to box in the Normans, forcing them to winter in place before fighting them off in the spring. With luck, the same worries over foodstuffs that were in the back of the minds of so many Englishmen would break the invader's back.

In the end, of course, we know the action Harold took. On hearing news of William's arrival, he turned his tired army on its heels and hastened south. By 6 October he was back in London, no doubt receiving detailed reports on William's position and actions. Some of our sources suggest there was an earnest debate about what to do: Orderic Vitalis says that Harold's brother, Gyrth, advised a slower pace to the response. More time meant a stronger, more rested army. Harold, though, had other ideas – among which was surely that he was flushed with victory. Just five days later, he was marching to meet the invader.

And on 14 October, they faced each other in the battle that would change everything.

Before we leave Hastings with William, however, a tour of Hastings Castle, which sits above the old town, is very much in order.

Hastings Castle
115 Castle Hill Road, Hastings TN34, UK
(lat. 50.8571, long. 0.5857)

Directions: From Pevensey, take the A2101 off the roundabout on the A259 in the centre of Hastings. Two right-hand turns will take you up Castle Hill Road; the footpath entrance to the site is near the top of the hill. Parking is available in public lots and along the streets surrounding West Hill. There is a nominal entrance fee to the site.

Some time after his victory at the Battle of Hastings, William ordered the building of Hastings Castle on the promontory of West Hill, atop the remains of an Iron Age hill fort. It was originally constructed as a motte-and-bailey castle: a wooden tower was built atop an earthen mound (motte) inside a courtyard (bailey) that was protected by a wooden palisade. Not long afterward, the wooden fortifications were ordered replaced by stone. In 1069, control of the castle was given to Robert, count of Eu, who a few years later founded the Collegiate

The motte of Hastings Castle, with what little remains of its once-imposing bailey. (*Michael Livingston*)

Church of St Mary-in-the-Castle, possibly replacing an earlier chapel on the site. Over time, the walls of this church were incorporated into the walls of the castle. These walls are some of the best preserved on the site today.

The great storms of the thirteenth century that reshaped so much of the coastline here not only effectively eradicated the port at Hastings, it also sent part of the castle's promontory into the sea – and the castle's keep with it. The economic strength of the town broken, there was little reason to restore its military strength. The church within its walls was dismantled with the Dissolution of the Monasteries in 1539.

What was left of the castle fell into ruin and over the years the site was used for farming, gardens, a tourist attraction and a position for artillery during the Second World War. Today, historical signage surrounds the limited remaining ruins and there are excellent panoramic views of Hastings and the sea.

A view from the top of the motte of Hastings Castle underscores the advantages of its location on the promontory. In the foreground are the remains of the church built within its walls. To the left are the beaches of Hastings, far below the sweep of cliff where the rest of the castle once stood. On the horizon is Pevensey, where William first arrived. (*Michael Livingston*)

To Battle

On or around 11 October, Harold marched out of London. To make speed, he might well have followed the Roman roads, just as he surely had in marching north. His fastest route in this case was to march from London to Rochester on Watling Street, roughly following the A2 today. From there he would have taken a smaller road south toward Hastings through Maidstone, Staplehurst and Bodiam – the A229 follows much of its route today. This road continues on through

Sedlescombe on the B2244, but as we will see Harold would have deviated from it at Cripps Corner, where he joined the Rye-Uckfield ridgeway to reach the site of the battle. Optional routes would have meant less-travelled roads: one ran from London to Lewes, from which Harold would have deviated onto the Uckfield-Rye ridgeway around Maresfield. Or perhaps the London-Rye road to likewise meet with the ridgeway.

We have so little data about the English movements at this point that we are unlikely to ever know the true path of Harold's march. If William's actions after the Battle of Hastings are indicative of his plans before the battle – that is, he was always planning to march east to secure the south-east before advancing up Watling Street to London – and Harold had any inkling of this then Harold's route would surely have been the Roman Road advancing to meet the same. If instead William had plans to move west, to make an attack on the ancient English capital at Winchester – or if Harold thought he planned to do so – then a more western route of approach would make more sense. We simply do not have enough information to say.

We can be certain, though, that at its heart Harold's plan was simple. He wanted to trap William and then put him into flight. If he could reach the Hastings peninsula before the Normans left it, he could manage to do just that – William could go nowhere but home from there. Throughout this march, then, Harold surely hoped that his speed would keep pace with the news of his march. He had surprised the invader two weeks earlier and destroyed them. He had the chance to do so again.

William, reacting to Harold's movements when at last he heard of them (more on this in the next chapter), had far less distance to travel. Gathering his men, he marched up onto the ridgeline above Hastings, where a trackway ran up the spine of the peninsula to meet with the same route Harold was marching down. If he had not done so in prior days, he may now have stopped at Old St Helen's Church, which today lies in ruins – though it is an open question whether it existed in Saxon times or dates to the immediate years after the Conquest.

For the 1066 tourist, this site can be visited on the drive from Hastings to Battle.

Old St Helen's Church
Ore Place, Hastings TN34, UK
(lat. 50.8792, long. 0.5865)

Directions: From Hastings Castle, take the A2101 north. Turn right on Elphinstone Road and follow it towards the ridgeline. Turn left on De Chardin Drive, the last left turn before the road terminates with the B2093. An immediate left turn on Centurion Rise will be followed by an immediate right turn onto Ore Place. The ruins are to the right. Parking is available along the street.

Of the seven medieval churches in Hastings, the storms that destroyed so much of the port and its landscape have left only two standing: All Saints and St Clements, neither of which seem to have

The ruins of Old St Helen's Church. (*Oliver Tookey*)

existed in William's day. Whether Old St Helen's Church, in nearby Ore, sits on the site of an earlier church is unknown, though it seems possible.

Though largely dismantled in the nineteenth century in order to provide the building materials for the new St Helen's Church in Ore, the ruins of Old St Helen's that remain incorporate an eleventh-century nave, a twelfth-century tower and a thirteenth-century chancel with the remains of a beautiful fourteenth-century window. The font also dates from the thirteenth century.

Hastings Museum and Art Gallery (Optional)
Bohemia Road, Hastings TN34, UK
(lat. 50.8565, long. 0.5709)

Directions: Beside the A21 atop the rising hill north-west of the centre of town.

Among the many pleasures awaiting visitors to Hastings, those in pursuit of its early years should consider a visit to the local history museum. It doesn't have a large medieval collection, but there are at least a few artefacts worth note, beginning with a silver penny of William I, struck at the Hastings mint. Also on display are the keys to Hastings Castle, a wine jug recovered from its grounds that dates from around 1100 and a thirteenth-century encaustic floor tile that was excavated from Old St Helen's Church in 2011.

Chapter 5

THE BATTLE OF HASTINGS

When it comes to the Battle of Hastings, perhaps no piece of evidence looms larger – figuratively and literally – than Battle Abbey. Now a Grade I English Heritage site, Battle Abbey is impossible to miss on the south side of the A2100 in the town of Battle: '1066 Battle of Hastings, Abbey and Battlefield', as the signs say. The site is a beautiful one and any 1066 tour *must* include it.

Before we get to our guide to the grounds of Battle Abbey, which appears below as Tour Five, we need to address the reason why this spot is so vital to 1066, the reason why it is traditionally identified as the location of the Battle of Hastings.

The story begins as the two armies approached each other. Part of William's claim against his adversary, as we have already discussed, was that Harold had broken a sacred oath. By the Norman accounting, not only was he unfit to rule as a result, but he was outright contemptible. Fighting against him thus took on a quasi-religious spirit.

Committing acts of war for a god of peace was hardly a new irony in 1066: there was already a long-standing precedent and procedure for how to sanctify the murder of fellow Christians and it began well before boots were on the ground. Achieving initial church sanction was obviously ideal and William had that. The papal banner he supposedly flew at the head of his army was every bit a part of his planning as the ships that had ferried them all across the English Channel. Having religious figures close beside him as the campaign unfolded was also essential. Learned men were useful advisors in any case, but having learned men who could bless decisions and reassure the men of their righteous cause was even better.

Odo of Bayeux

One of the most important of William's advisors in 1066 was his half-brother on his mother's side, Odo of Bayeux. Duke William made him bishop of Bayeux in 1049, when Odo was perhaps still a teenager – it's always been good to have friends in high places, it seems – and he used his resources to support William's claim to the English throne. This meant financial support in providing ships for the invasion fleet, but it also meant Odo himself, who rode at his half-brother's side throughout the campaign. He is featured a few times in the Bayeux Tapestry, which many scholars believe was commissioned by him in England (executed almost certainly in Canterbury) and then taken to his cathedral in Bayeux.

In the immediate years after Hastings William named Odo the earl of Kent and entrusted him with the regency of the kingdom when he was away on the Continent. Despite this trust, he would later come into disrepute for alledged misappropriation of Church lands. And, after William's death, he would help lead an unsuccessful rebellion on behalf of William's eldest son – Robert Curthose, who succeeded his father as duke of Normandy – against William's second-oldest – William Rufus, who succeeded his father as king of England.

Bishop Odo blesses a meal before the Battle of Hastings, from the Bayeux Tapestry. (*Musée de la Tapisserie de Bayeux*)

There is a story, related in a charter of Battle Abbey, that William's religious fervour was such that he proclaimed before the battle in 1066 that he would build a great monastery on the site of his victory. A fine story, to be sure, except that the charter in question is a forgery of 1154!

Still, it may be that William recognized early on that part of his repayment for the support of the church would be the building of one. Building churches had been part of how he had achieved sanction for his marriage; doing so to achieve sanction for his conquest cannot have been a great leap of logic. Promising such a construction might also have bolstered the spirit of his own men rallying behind him, giving them promises of rewards both earthly and divine. Further on, building a church specifically upon the battlefield to pray for the souls of those who died for and against him would certainly be an elegant solution to an enormous problem that faced the duke: turning the English people into loyal subjects despite what he may have done to their fathers, brothers and sons upon the field. The promise to establish a monastery was certainly made by 1070, when the Papacy suggested as much and William was a man of his word. As the *Anglo-Saxon Chronicle* records, 'On the very spot where God granted him the conquest of England he caused a great abbey to be built; and settled monks in it and richly endowed it'.

Or, more accurately said, he carried through with ordering others to build one. There is no indication that William, once he left the field of the battle of Hastings, ever returned to it. The religious establishment he ordered built – not just a church of commemoration, but an abbey – was begun around 1071, but it was his son, William Rufus, who dedicated it in 1094, seven years after the Conqueror's death.

According to a twelfth-century chronicle written at Battle Abbey, William did keep tabs on the progress of the project, however. Among his standing orders was that the abbey would be built on the very ground of the battle itself. This matches the information provided by William of Malmesbury, writing around 1125, who states that the abbey 'is called Battle Abbey because the principal church is to be seen on the very spot where, according to tradition, among the piled heaps of corpses Harold was found'. The same is reported from various other contemporary writers and little evidence has ever been presented to think they all mislead.

Battle Abbey Relics

Like many medieval churches, Battle Abbey housed a number of relics, physical artefacts connected with Christian saints. Among those relics housed in a golden, gem-covered container within the abbey were pieces of the True Cross and Christ's Tomb, as well as hair that was believed to have belonged to the Apostles Peter and Paul.

Thus it is, as we will see momentarily as we conduct a tour of its grounds, that today there sits a stone marker on the grasses where once stood the high altar of the abbey's church, marking the spot where the body of Harold was found. That placement fixes the end of the battle upon a ridgeline and the imagination begins to fill in the battle accordingly: William's troops rushing up the long slope of open ground that stretches to the south and east, all of them converging upon some last stand here, where died the last Anglo-Saxon king of England. Yet there are many people who doubt whether this is indeed the location where Harold's body was found.

That there should be doubt about Battle Abbey's claim to be associated with the Battle of Hastings is at once both understandable and astonishing. On the one hand, no archaeological evidence of a great battle has been found on the site. On the other hand, if the abbey is not associated with the famous battle, why on earth is it there?

The site, after all, is not a good one. Ideally, a medieval abbey required several things: fields for flocks and crops, ponds for fish and, perhaps most vitally, a supply of clean water. Battle Abbey, perched atop a rocky ridgeline, had effectively none of them. Even worse, the slope of the ground was so uneven that the work of constructing a functional church carried with it additional difficulties.

Something of this final trouble is still visible at the site today. Though the abbey's great church and other buildings are gone, its impressive dormitory remains. Beyond the haunting beauty of this roofless ruin, an observer can see at a glance that this structure, which served as a common living and sleeping space for the abbey's monks, required a good bit of planning to construct. Most obviously, a look at its sides reveals how its constructors were forced to grapple with the sloping ground around the ridge: to achieve a level floor,

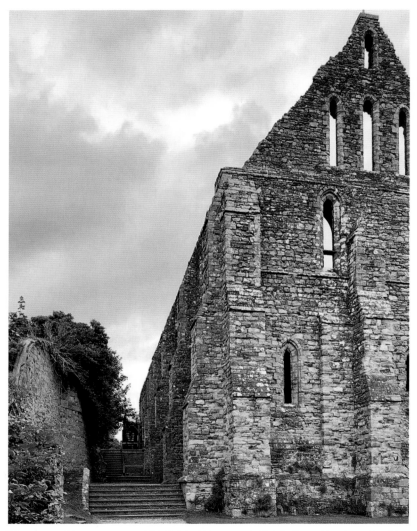

The slope of the mount on which Battle Abbey was built is indicated by the stairs rising beside the monk's dormitory and the significant buttressing required to support the tall facade. (*Michael Livingston*)

the southern end of the dormitory has to rise substantially farther off the ground than the northern end. Taller walls meant thicker walls, more work and more buttressing just to keep them from collapsing outward from their own weight.

Benedictine Monks

Battle Abbey followed the Rule of St Benedict, which dictated everything from the daily rituals of the monks to the arrangement of their monastery buildings. This strict regulation followed the monks in everything they did, including in their diet: since fish was the only meat they could eat during Lent, close proximity to fish ponds was a must-have for the medieval monk!

There is a pond for both fish and fresh water down the southern slope of the ridge. A cleared greensward and marked paths run down to it today, often strewn with milling sheep, but this would not have been the case when the abbey was being sited. Back then, if a person had any sense at all, one imagines they would have placed the abbey in closer proximity to the water, where there were flatter building sites and even better shelter from the wind. All logic says Battle Abbey should not have been built where it was.

Unless, of course, it *had* to be built here because William ordered it to be built upon the site of his victory and, quite simply, this is it.

Numerous alternative locations have nevertheless been put forward over the years, largely due to the lack of archaeological evidence found at this site. In no case, however, has any alternative thus far presented found acceptance in the scholarly community. Like the traditional site, none has confirming archaeological evidence; unlike it, they often don't make sense in light of our textual evidence. Thus, while we cannot categorically deny other possibilities, it is our position that, barring the revelation of physical remains, the abbey's location is too difficult to explain away as anything but what it is reported to be: the site of William's victory in 1066.

That said, even if we were *completely* certain that the battle took place in association with this spot, we cannot be entirely certain *how*. Because archaeological investigations have uncovered no battle-related remains that would enable us to confidently identify the location or direction of fighting, we are left only with those clues we can derive from the landscape, from our understandings of warfare in the period and from our sources.

Visitors to the site of Battle Abbey today – Tour Four, below – will be presented with an interpretation that we will here call the 'traditional' interpretation of Hastings: the high altar of the abbey marks the site of Harold's death, with his battle lines running east-west across the grounds south of this spot. William and the Normans would be in their own east-west lines down and around the valley below, making the battle itself take place on a north-south basis.

We see significant difficulties in this 'traditional' interpretation. While we accept the veracity of the abbey's location, we favour instead what we will here call a 'modified' positioning of the lines that makes the battle take place on a more east-west basis. Both the 'traditional' and 'modified' interpretations are outlined in the tour provided here.

First, however, it is important to understand what our sources tell us about the battle, beginning with the arms and armour the men used.

Weapons and Armour

The Bayeux Tapestry is not only a unique historical survival, but it also provides a wonderfully clear depiction of the arms and armour used in Western Europe in the second half of the eleventh century; among many other things, it depicts over 200 armed men of whom 79 are also wearing mail armour. By the eleventh century, these were called hauberks. Worn by both cavalry and infantry, the hauberk was a mail shirt reaching to the knees with short sleeves made all in one piece as indicated along the tapestry's border of corpses being stripped of their armour by pulling it over their heads – also an indication of the continued value of the armour. The hauberk was probably worn over, but not attached to, a heavy quilted undergarment, the haubergeon, which added to the defensive capability of the armour, although this is not depicted in the Tapestry. Most hauberks in the Bayeux Tapestry are shown descending to the knees and divided down the front and back to allow greater freedom of movement and comfort, especially on horseback. One figure is depicted with a long-sleeved hauberk, but most have short, wide sleeves, which leave the forearms bare. Coloured bands along the edges of the sleeves and skirt may mean that cloth was sewn onto these to soften the roughness of the metal and to guard against irritation. One horseman is also depicted with

This depiction of the Norman cavalry from the Bayeux Tapestry shows the armour that was worn and weapons carried at the Battle of Hastings. (*Musée de la Tapisserie de Bayeux*)

additional protection for the forearms, although most are shown with no further protection for the arms or hands. Similarly, very few soldiers wear armour on their legs, although some leaders and other important soldiers, including both William the Conqueror and Harold Godwinson, have mail leggings (or chausses). Other figures, again mostly leaders or important soldiers, are shown wearing a mail hood or coif over which their helmet fits. Whether this was connected to the hauberk or was an additional piece of mail, like the chausses, is unclear. Finally, several soldiers, all Norman horsemen, including William the Conqueror, have coloured rectangles on the breasts of their hauberks. These are most likely mail ventails (the face covering of a mail coif), which are unlaced for comfort when not in battle.

All the helmets shown in the Tapestry are of the same pattern: a close-fitting conical helmet with a somewhat pointed apex and a wide, flat nasal guard attached to the brim and descending down over the nose. While not depicted in the Bayeux Tapestry, other artistic sources from the period show that these helmets were secured in place with a leather strap tied under the chin. All of the helmets appear to have been made from a single piece of iron forged into shape, although it is possible that some were made of several pieces of iron attached together – spangenhelms.

The shields depicted on the Bayeux Tapestry, whether carried by infantry or cavalry, are almost all kite shields, long and narrow, rounded over the top and coming to a point at the bottom. Some appear to curve slightly, although how much and whether all kite shields had this characteristic cannot be determined. These were made of wood covered with leather, a metal boss and perhaps a metal rim, although this latter is impossible to ascertain from the Tapestry alone. The shields are shown held in a variety of ways by leather straps (or enarmes) riveted onto their inside. When not used, they are carried by a loose strap draped around the soldier's neck and under an arm. The Tapestry shows that the kite shield allowed foot soldiers to plant the sharper bottom edge into the ground and, by overlapping the wider upper part of each shield, form the shield wall. The shield was also frequently decorated, although there seems to be no consistency in their patterns – and the late eleventh century is too early for heraldry. Among the designs which appear are birds, dragons, wavy crosses, diagonal lines and saltires, with the boss and rivets also sometimes incorporated into the pattern. Some of the

An axe and sword, from the Bayeux Tapestry. (*Musée de la Tapisserie de Bayeux*)

English infantry carry round shields and there is a single rectangular shield, also carried by an English foot soldier.

The weapons carried by the soldiers on the Bayeux Tapestry include spears, swords, axes and maces/clubs. The spear was the most prominent weapon in the premodern world. It required little training to use and was versatile, in that it could be used as a thrusting weapon by both cavalry and infantry or thrown. All three of these can be seen in the Tapestry. Spears also could be of different lengths, although all in the Tapestry seem to be the same. The swords depicted are also all of similar length and show no special construction or ornamentation. Axes, all of which appear to be held in English hands, were common among Northern Europe lands settled by Vikings. Although there were two common types of Viking battleaxes – the *skeggφx* or bearded axe, because its blade was drawn down like a beard, and the *breidφx* or broad axe, which had a more triangular-shaped head – all in the Tapestry appear to be the latter. The Tapestry is the first artistic representation of maces. Although some have interpreted the short-handled, bulbous-headed weapons depicted – one carried by William, one by Odo and one flying through the air – to be simple clubs, the odd shapes at the end are more likely interpreted as separate heads secured to wooden sticks.

What We Know of the Battle

Our sources – most importantly the contemporary chronicler William of Poitiers, the poetic *Carmen* by Guy of Amiens and the remarkable Bayeux Tapestry – provide some essential elements to the battle.

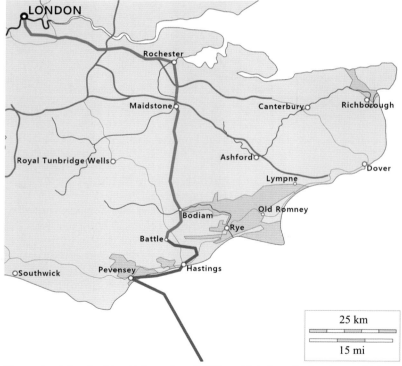

The routes taken by Harold (green) and William (violet) to the battle, overlaid over the major towns and roads of the modern landscape. (*Michael Livingston*)

Each side probably had roughly 5,000 to 7,000 men. The English army had moved with considerable speed since their victory at Stamford Bridge far to the north, as the previous chapter has shown. They were undoubtedly exhausted.

Medieval commanders often utilized the old Roman roads to speed their movements across the landscape and the main Roman route from London to Hastings would have run through Sedlescombe (see Tour Five, below). To save time and keep his forces as fresh as he could, Harold may well have followed these roads most of the way to the coast.

As it happens, Battle Abbey is not on this Roman road, but upon a smaller, likely less-travelled ridgeway that followed the high ground around Sedlescombe. One explanation could be that the Roman road was impassable in 1066 due to heavy rains in the valley, perhaps even a broken bridge over the River Brede. But we have no evidence for this whatsoever. A simpler explanation, then, could be that Harold specifically chose the less-travelled route in order to approach the invading forces from an unexpected direction. He would surprise William just as he had surprised Harald Hardrada and Tostig.

The Normans ride out from their beachhead, from the Bayeux Tapestry. (*Musée de la Tapisserie de Bayeux*)

According to William of Poitiers, the plan almost worked: as the English approached, many of the Normans were out foraging. But William's scouts located the coming army and he was able to gather

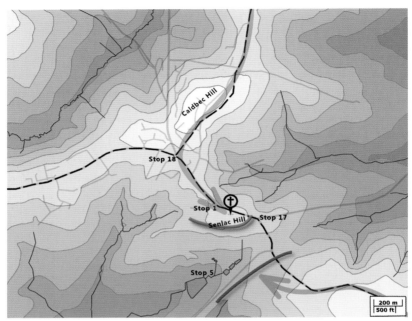

The location of the High Altar of Battle Abbey and stops on our tour overlaid upon the traditional interpretation of the Battle of Hastings. The approximate locations of the medieval paths are shown as dashed lines, superimposed on the modern roads of the town of Battle. The English (green) approach from the north to take position on Senlac Hill, surrounding Harold's standard at or near the Battle Abbey church. The Normans (violet) approach from the south-east, taking position to charge uphill into the English shield-wall. (*Michael Livingston*)

his own to march out to meet it. On the night of 13 October, the two forces made camp within sight of each other, preparing for the battle in the morning.

The English had the higher ground: their scouts had likely brought word of the Norman march in turn and Harold had wisely taken the position most conducive to the forming of his shield-wall. This was a tried and true tactic of warfare among the English: dismounted, they would close ranks with overlapping shields and brandished spears. In their centre was Harold and his fierce huscarls, all armed with axes.

William is notified of Harold's approach, from the Bayeux Tapestry. (*Musée de la Tapisserie de Bayeux*)

Like the Macedonian phalanx of old, the shield-wall was a formation that was both simple to assemble and proven to be highly effective against the cavalry charges that the Normans were expected to employ. Like its ancient counterpart, however, its primary weakness was its general lack of manoeuvrability. That the English appear to have chosen the battlefield was thus an early victory: their shield-wall was, generally speaking, a defensive-minded tactic best suited for a fixed position on contested ground. Higher ground and the Norman willingness to attack gave them just that.

If Harold's intent in hurrying had been to bottle up the Normans, to trap them on the Hastings peninsula, his speed had managed just that. He had reached the bottleneck. His shields were the cork. All he had to do was hold.

Facing them, William separated his army into three major units. At his left wing were the Breton troops who had accompanied him. At his right wing were the Flemings and Boulognese – the *Carmen* calls these, collectively, the French. In the centre, under his own command, were his Normans. Lines of bowmen were up front. The second rank were stronger and better armoured foot soldiers, according to William of Poitiers. Behind them all were the lines of Norman heavy cavalry, which were a few thousand strong.

After the lines had formed up, war cries resounded over the field as the two armies made displays of aggression that were intended to intimidate their enemy while boosting their own morale. The field would have been a roiling mix of rage and roar, calls and the clashing of steel.

It was at this point, the *Carmen* says, 'while the martial engagements hung with uncertainty and the bitter scourge of death by spears was eminent', that a Norman mummer named Taillefer emerged from the lines and made a show of juggling his sword while on horseback. When an Englishman walked out to fight him – this was, after all, just one more signal of aggression – the Norman rode him down and ran him through with his lance. Dismounting, Taillefer quickly beheaded the man and held the bloody trophy up for both lines to see. It was around 9 in the morning and the first blood of Hastings had been spilled.

Trumpets signalled the initial major action: an exchange of ranged attacks. The invaders shot arrows. The English responded with arrows, spears and other missiles. The Norman infantry were hard-pressed as they fought toward the higher ground.

The initial Norman attacks, from the Bayeux Tapestry. (*Musée de la Tapisserie de Bayeux*)

Our sources agree that after some time of this struggle, the Norman lines had gained no ground. As the men on foot disengaged, the Normans sent forward men on horseback to make a mounted assault on the shield-wall: 'those who had been in the rear found themselves in the front', William of Poitiers writes, and soon 'the great war-cries' that each side had been shouting 'were drowned by the noise of battle and the groans of the dying'.

This assault, too, was repulsed. The English line, according to the *Carmen*, was a 'dense forest', so tightly packed that the dead were held upright by being pressed up among the living. William of Poitiers says much the same thing: there was no room for the men to fall. Added to their advantage in position, the thickness of the English lines was an enormous obstacle to any attempt to overrun them. The shield-wall would have seemed an immovable object.

The Bayeux Tapestry shows Harold's brothers, the Earls Gyrth and Leofwine, being cut down while surrounded in what appears

The English shield-wall repulses the initial attacks, from the Bayeux Tapestry. (*Musée de la Tapisserie de Bayeux*)

The English lines take multiple attacks, but the king's banner still flies. (*Musée de la Tapisserie de Bayeux*)

to be this early phase of the battle. We have no idea if this was so. William of Poitiers doesn't say when or by whom the brothers were killed during the day's fighting – only that they died. The *Carmen* has Gyrth dying at William's own hand just before he personally takes part in the killing of Harold much later in the battle – a rather improbable tale, as we will see.

If the two earls *did* die early in the day, it would certainly go some way toward explaining the subsequent events of the battle: they were undoubtedly Harold's most valuable lieutenants on the field. Losing them meant losing an essential component of command and control across his lines and few things can be more disastrous to an army in an engagement.

The earls Gyrth and Leofwine are killed, from the Bayeux Tapestry. (*Musée de la Tapisserie de Bayeux*)

When the assaults against the English shield-wall failed to break it, the *Carmen* says the invaders tried a feigned retreat: 'The French, versed in stratagems, skilled in warfare, pretended to fly as if defeated.' Tactically, this was intended to provoke the enemy to break ranks in pursuit of those thought to be retreating; at a signal, those retreating would turn, form up and destroy their pursuers away from their defensive lines. Because so much of the manoeuvre depends on timing, communications and the ability of soldiers to follow commands in the heat of battle, it is among the more difficult tactics to attempt in the field.

Slaughter on both sides, from the Bayeux Tapestry. (*Musée de la Tapisserie de Bayeux*)

For the Normans, the *Carmen* reports that the stratagem worked. A portion of the English line pursued the fleeing men. They were predictably slaughtered when the invaders turned back around – the poem says 10,000 died, which is poetic licence, to be sure – but the English who'd stayed in their lines didn't despair or panic. If anything, they 'attacked more furiously and counted their losses nothing'. Thus, the *Carmen* says, the Norman lines as a whole were sent into a retreat that was not feigned.

William of Poitiers contradicts the *Carmen* quite clearly here, claiming that there was nothing at all feigned about this first retreat. Instead, he writes, the 'ferocity' of the English resistance simply

Men are falling, but the English lines on the high ground are holding, from the Bayeux Tapestry. (*Musée de la Tapisserie de Bayeux*)

The Normans retreat from the English lines. (*Musée de la Tapisserie de Bayeux*)

William lifts his helm, showing that he still lives and halting the retreat of his men. (*Musée de la Tapisserie de Bayeux*)

caused the infantry and cavalry on the Norman left wing to start to give way. Perhaps sparked by this action, a rumour spread through the rest of the attacking lines that William himself had been killed. The whole left wing started to fall back. The Norman centre followed suit. An unorganized retreat began.

The chronicler tries to put the best spin on this he can: because they thought their leader dead, 'their retreat wasn't a shameful flight but a sorrowful withdrawal'. For its part, the *Carmen* says nothing of the sort. It describes the invaders as 'vanquished': 'The Normans fled', he says, 'their shields covered their backs!'

The whole invasion was faltering. And, despite their differences, William of Poitiers, the *Carmen* and the Bayeux Tapestry all agree on what happened in this perilous moment. The duke rode at once among his retreating forces, pulling his helm back from his face so that could be seen. Re-organizing the ranks – the sources have him using a mix of inspiration and outright threats – William stopped the retreat and sent his men forward again.

A number of Harold's men had been drawn out from the shield-wall, trying to run down the fleeing invaders. Some were caught in the open and destroyed. The rest fell back and a melee once more unfolded at the shield-wall as the Normans tried to press through the gaps that Harold was trying to close.

It was now, William of Poitiers says, that the Normans attempted a feigned retreat: 'They remembered how, a little earlier, flight had led to the success they desired.' As they executed the same manoeuvre, great numbers of the English accordingly rushed forward. The Normans then spun, 'stopped them on their tracks, crushed them completely and massacred them down to the last man'.

William of Poitiers relates that they 'twice used this trick with the same success', which seems to say that there were three total retreats (one real, two tricks), though one could possibly argue he means just two (one real that turned to good, one trick). The *Carmen* has two retreats (one trick, one real), but it is difficult to square the idea that the Normans were well-trained in the stratagem of a feigned retreat with the idea that they could turn so quickly in panic. The story told by William of Poitiers – that William decided to use the tactic on the field – makes the most sense.

The Bayeux Tapestry can be a Rorschach Test of sorts – we tend to see in it what we want to see – but it arguably has something like William of Poitiers' version of events. After the early deaths of Gyrth and Leofwine, there is a long sequence of violent events, with Norman cavalry attacking Englishmen on a hill. Two of these riders appear to be dying in water, which (as we will see on touring the site, below) could indicate their presence on the left wing. Cavalry are then shown moving into what appears to be a chaotic retreat.

In the middle of the retreat, Bishop Odo is pictured on horseback, wielding a club. The embroidered wording above him says that he 'gives strength to the boys' – the final word (*puros* in Latin) perhaps a not-too-subtle dig at the manhood of those whose flight he was trying to stop. William then appears, lifting his helm and pushing the forces back into action. As with the other sources, the Normans then savage those English units who had broken from the shield-wall in pursuit of the retreating men.

Whether the feigned retreats are a propagandist spin on a reality of multiple unorganized retreats or evidence of a remarkable tactical

The Normans strike the thinning English shield-wall, from the Bayeux Tapestry. (*Musée de la Tapisserie de Bayeux*)

adjustment on the field, the results were the same. Each retreating action encouraged portions of the English lines to break ranks and descend from the shield-wall after them only to be cut down as the Normans spun around and reformed their offensive attacks. Whether it was two or three or more such actions is perhaps irrelevant. The English lines were being whittled down.

The Normans now sent up more ranged attacks upon the shrinking and weakening shield-wall. And again and again the cavalry rode forth. It must have seemed that it was only a matter of time.

William of Poitiers is noticeably silent on the means of Harold's death, which has led some to suspect that something about his killing made the chronicler uncomfortable – perhaps an action not in keeping with his efforts to portray William as a righteous and just man. The most popular image of the king's death thus comes from the depiction of a man on the Bayeux Tapestry being struck by an arrow to the eye below the caption '*Hic Harold rex interfectus est*' [Here King Harold had been killed]. But this man is almost assuredly not Harold. And the arrow to the unknown fellow's eye appears to be a mistaken alteration to the tapestry that dates to the first decades of the nineteenth century. Instead, the English king is more likely the next man on the tapestry: an axeman falling beneath the sword-stroke of a Norman knight.

This would fit with the story told in the *Carmen*, which has William late in the day personally leading a mounted charge against the English. His horse is struck down beneath him, felled by a spear thrown by Harold's brother, Gyrth. The duke fights on by foot and kills Gyrth. He then seizes another horse and fights on again before

Harold dies. But which man is Harold? (*Musée de la Tapisserie de Bayeux*)

this mount, too, is taken out from beneath him by a spear throw. Once more William kills his attacker on foot. Now Eustace II of Boulogne arrives and gives William his horse. One of Eustace's knights lends his to his lord, in turn, and the two lords press on toward Harold's standard. William strikes the king first, his lance punching through Harold's chest. Eustace runs his blade across his neck, below the protection of his helm. Two more Normans follow close behind. Hugh de Ponthieu's lance finds Harold's stomach. A man named Gifford severs Harold's leg and carries it off as a trophy.

All told, this is a dramatic sequence – a bit too dramatic and laudatory of the Norman leadership, one might say. Yet the idea that the king was hacked down makes sense of what we glean of the end of the battle. The shield-wall was collapsing and Norman riders would have been breaking through what remained – their every aim on the English standard and the man fighting beside it. However Harold fell, his loyal huscarls would have gone down around him, trying in vain to protect the king.

As the daylight faded, the English king and two earls were dead. William had dealt an extraordinary blow to the Godwin family and thereby the leadership of England.

Contrary to Hollywood's tendency to depict medieval battles as long affairs, they were, in truth, more usually short. Most engagements might best be counted in minutes before they ended in a bloody rout when one of the sides wavered and fled at the earliest hint of a loss of strength or heart. That Hastings was a battle counted in so many hours speaks volumes about how strong the English line was and how stout their resolve to defend their lands against the foreign invader must have been.

Now, with darkness giving hope of safety, the remaining English finally broke and fled for their lives. William of Poitiers writes of 'corpses all along the roads' as the Norman forces, 'although they did not know the countryside, pursued them eagerly'.

William of Poitiers writes of a last stand made by some of the English in 'a deep valley' with 'numerous ditches'. Other sources write of pursuing Normans dying when they rode into a single deep ditch that they could not see in the dark, which was later called 'malfosse'. Though many theories have been put forward for its location, but not one has revealed evidence of conflict. The site – if it existed – may well be considered lost.

The Tapestry breaks off with the Normans in pursuit of the fleeing English. How much further the embroidery would have taken the story is not known. (*Musée de la Tapisserie de Bayeux*)

What happened to the fallen is not known for certain, but it seems likely that while William buried his own dead, he made no effort to bury those of the English. Their rotting corpses were left as a sign for those who opposed him. As related in the introduction to this book, there are many stories regarding the fate of Harold's body. Quietly buried near the sea, as William of Poitiers and the *Carmen* relate. Taken and buried north of London at Waltham, as that abbey's chronicle claimed. Or even, as some still think, taken and buried in Bosham Church some 75 miles (121km) to the west, where a stone coffin with a headless, legless man was discovered in 1954.

Where William went afterwards will be covered in the next chapter. For now, however, let us examine the ground where tradition says Harold died and William won his crown.

TOUR FOUR: BATTLE ABBEY AND SURROUNDS

1066 Battle of Hastings, Abbey and Battlefield
Butter Cross, High St, Battle TN33 0AD, UK
(lat. 50.913708, long. 0.488447)
Entrance fee required

Directions: from Hastings, take the B2093 north to Battle. The abbey is on the south end of High Street in Battle. A large car park that provides ample off-street parking can be located in an associated ticket-controlled lot.

1 *The Great Gatehouse*
Dominating the visitor's approach to the site is the magnificent Great Gatehouse, which was built beginning in 1338 and served as the primary point of entry for all visitors to the abbey: those on foot entered through the smaller gateway, while those on horse or cart entered through the larger one. The structure, like the rest of the abbey, is built of local sandstone. The porter's room was through

The Great Gatehouse remains an impressive sight today. The former Courthouse attached to its left side is now the entrance to the site. (*Michael Livingston*)

the door in the west wall of the smaller passage. Beside the porter's accommodation on the ground floor are remains of the original gatehouse from the eleventh century. Above the main passageways in the gatehouse is a great chamber accessible by a stairway in the south-east turret. In the stairwell and chamber are visible remains of the defences built into the gatehouse: a portcullis and two murder-holes.

2 The Courthouse

The main entrance point for visitors today is the Courthouse that was appended to the gatehouse in the middle of the sixteenth century. This part of the structure incorporates earlier buildings on the site – likely including the abbey's almoner – that in places go back to the eleventh century. The courthouse was restored in the 1990s to serve as a well-appointed English Heritage gift shop selling Hastings memorabilia alongside local artisanal items.

3 The Visitor Centre

After paying visitor's fees at the gift shop and gathering supplies dependent on the weather, the visitor will enter the Battle Abbey grounds proper.

The immediate buildings beyond the gatehouse belong to the independent, co-educational Battle Abbey School. These buildings remain in use during the school year and are not typically open for tours. These will be discussed below.

Outside of the school buildings, visitors to the site are free to move through the grounds in whatever manner seems fit. Signage, however, does highlight potential routes depending on how long one intends to stay. The longest route loops around the traditional site of the battlefield before moving through the abbey grounds. This loop provides several vistas back up at the abbey buildings – as well as a good look at the traditional site of the battle and it is the tour outlined and recommended here. For those who will have difficulty making the full loop of roughly 1.2 miles (2km) due to physical or environmental troubles, however, a shorter route of 0.6 miles (1km) is recommended.

As a first stop all visitors should turn right after entering the grounds and walk along the inside of the Great Gatehouse. Down the slope to west here is an excellent Visitor Centre featuring a cafe, toilets, an exhibition area and a room largely dedicated to introducing visitors to the battle via a short film and hands-on recreations that children can enjoy.

From the visitor centre, a shaded path leads south for roughly 110 yards (100m) to a junction with an east-west road at the western end of the abbey's terrace. Those wishing to take the longer walk can proceed ahead, following the marked path down the wide slope and the immediate stops below. Those wishing for a shorter walk can follow this east-west road along the edge of the terrace to a gate at the farther corner of the abbey ruins, east of this location. Going this direction will pick up the tour at Stop 6, below – and not to worry, everything passed will be seen on the way back!

4 The Traditional Battlefield

The path, running south, dips through trees before opening out onto the grassy, sloping ground that is the west side of the 'traditional' battlefield. Though today this land is grazed by a flock of sheep, signage and other elements encourage visitors to imagine William's forces marching up the slope toward Harold's shield-wall nearer the top of the hill.

Down the slope, the path passes around a small pond and then up a small hillock that, in the view of many who hold to the 'traditional' reconstruction, marks the spot where English forces were caught on one of the occasions when they broke ranks from their shield-wall in an attempt to run down William's retreating left wing. This hillock as it stands today, however, dates from the eighteenth century.

5 The Valley Bottom

The path runs southward from here toward a large pond at the valley's bottom that was dug in the nineteenth century. To the left of the path, slightly up-slope, are three significantly smaller ponds that were utilized as fish ponds for the medieval abbey. Whether ponds of some sort pre-dated the abbey in this location is unknown, but the combined presence of all this water along the valley bottom suggests that the ground here would have been soft if not downright boggy in October 1066. The movements of men and horses – not to mention the liquids of blood, urine and excrement that come with battle –

would have worsened these conditions considerably. Walking the field today, therefore, it might be most appropriate to imagine these wetter areas marking the western reaches of William's lines rather than, as the traditional accounts would have it, the heart of them.

Crossing to the other side of the valley, the path swings around the medieval fish ponds and provides excellent views across the slopes toward the abbey above. The Norman lines, by our accounting, are likely to have run along the front face of the slope on this southeast side of the site, roughly parallel to Powdermill Lane (B2095), the road just beyond the fences to the visitor's right. A visit to the Roundabout outside the Abbey site (Stop 17) will provide a vantage point for this alternative siting of the battle.

From here the path runs up the slopes to a gate at the foot of the abbey remains, where those who chose a shorter examination of the site will join the tour.

The large pond that sits in the valley bottom today. (*Michael Livingston*)

The slope of open field where the Battle of Hastings is traditionally located, with Battle Abbey atop the hill. To the left is the heavy growth of tree and brush around the first of the small ponds that sit in the valley bottom. (*Michael Livingston*)

6 The East Range

The ruined walls facing the east-west road here are what remains of the monastery's East Range. The ghosts of its three storeys can be seen on the interior of its west (left) side: two arched doorways near the top of the wall mark the entrances to the abbey's main dormitory – the peaked structure that dominates the site (Stop 11, below). This level of the range would have held a long row of latrines.

Below these two high doorways are the traces of barrel vaulting over a larger doorway. This level was an extended dormitory. A smaller doorway at this same level would have led to a second row of latrines.

The ground level, with its large arched entrances would have been storage spaces and rooms for novice monks. On this ground floor can be seen the remains of the latrine drain. Among the many reasons the monks would have desired a location closer to water than the barren hilltop would have been the fact that running water could have been run through channels on the site to make relatively quick work of flushing the latrines. Lacking this, the monks would have been forced to clean the latrines with shovels and buckets. A vile task indeed!

The East Range of the abbey, with the Dormitory behind it. (*Michael Livingston*)

7 *The Dairy and Icehouse*
Continuing north from the gate, visitors will pass by a walled garden that sits to the right side of the East Range before encountering the Dairy, a small octagonal building with a thatched roof to the left. This structure (restored in 1991) and the small, underground Icehouse beside it are both unlikely survivals of the early nineteenth century: winter ice could be stored in the Icehouse to use in summer months. The Dairy is built in the Gothic style to mimic the abbey. When the abbey was still functioning, this was the site of its infirmary.

8 *The Abbey Church*
The path winds north-west to the site of the Abbey Church, now a foundational footprint in the ground. The building itself was

The exposed crypt of the expanded abbey church. (*Michael Livingston*)

destroyed in 1538, one of many victims of Henry VIII's Dissolution of the Monasteries, a systematic disbanding of monastic properties after his declaration of English independence from the Catholic Church. A sandstone plaque in the ground marks the presumed location of the church's high altar – by tradition the site where King Harold died, around which the entirety of the abbey has been situated.

Marked on the ground is the outline of the original church, completed in 1094, which was roughly 225ft (68m) in length. Almost 200 years later, the east end of the church was demolished and greatly expanded by a monumental seven-bay choir capped with radiating chapels; the church was now over 300ft (92m) in length. A vaulted crypt, made necessary by the slope, provided room for three more chapels on a lower level. This crypt, excavated in 1817, remains open to the elements today.

9 *The Precinct Wall*

North of the Abbey Church is a stretch of stone wall that dates from the first quarter of the twelfth century. This Precinct Wall would have marked the line of the abbey's immediate grounds, separating it off for both privacy and protection. The west end of this wall, close to the Great Gatehouse, is built with the additional defensive feature of a wall-walk. This unusual feature for an abbey likely dates from the

Wall walks such as this are common sights in castles, but they are a much rarer sight at an abbey. (*Kelly DeVries*)

fourteenth century, when the gatehouse was refashioned beginning in 1338.

10 The Chapter House
Directly beside the south transept of the Abbey Church, beside the path followed up from the Dairy, are the excavated ruins of the Chapter House. Though a simple building in terms of architecture, the chapter house held an absolutely central role in the life of the monks at Battle Abbey. Each day they would have come to this building, both to hear the daily reading of the Benedictine Rule that organized their daily tasks and responsibilities and to discuss community matters.

11 The Dormitory
The abbey's Dormitory was originally its second-largest building. Today, with the Abbey Church destroyed, this surviving ruin absolutely dominates the visual impression of the entire site. Though roofless since the late eighteenth century – and missing the entirety of its northern end – the Dormitory's scope is readily recognizable by the magnificent peak of its remaining southern end, complete with the extensive buttressing made necessary by the uneven slopes on the hilltop.

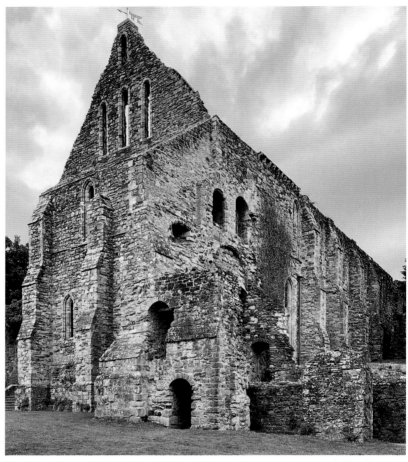

The Dormitory of Battle Abbey. (*Michael Livingston*)

The top level of this building was where most of the abbey's monks slept in simple beds along the walls. (A smaller number would have slept in the dormitory of the connected East Range seen in Stop 6.) While originally constructed as an open, communal space, there are indications that dividing partitions were put in place in the fifteenth

The Dormitory, viewed from the site of the church. The two levels of its construction can be seen. (*Michael Livingston*)

Even stripped of their plaster and paint, the stone pillars and ribbing beneath the Dormitory are an impressive sight. (*Michael Livingston*)

century. Close examination of the stone of some window openings reveals traces of white plaster with thin lines of red paint. Such decoration, meant to mimic the appearance of expensive masonry work, is thought to have covered the entirety of the walls in this space – as well as those in other parts of the abbey.

Below the dormitory space is a connected series of chambers, beginning with the Novice's Chamber on the south end. The soaring interior height of this room once again underscores the slope of the ground on the hilltop – a point in favour of this being the ground of the battle, as discussed above.

The use of the next chamber to the north is unknown, but the next one – a smaller, barrel-vaulted passage – was the slype, a passageway between the cloister to the west (Stop 12) and the Infirmary to the east, where the Dairy and Icehouse now stand (Stop 7).

To the north of the slype is a room that is believed to have served as the monks' Common Room. The relatively lower ceiling here provides an excellent opportunity for visitors to see the extraordinary engineering work necessary to hold the weight of the large stone and wood Dormitory above. The columns here are marble, matched by carefully carved corbels that connect the vaults onto the walls. Likewise impressive are the lancet windows spread across the eastern wall.

The final room beneath the Dormitory is a small one at its northern end. This is believed to have been the Inner Parlour. It was general practice for monks to engage in as few conversations as possible – their minds, of course, were supposed to be on higher matters – but when a talk was necessary this was the place to do it. The small size and simplicity of the room speak volumes (if you'll forgive the pun) about the little volume they were expected to speak!

12 *The Cloister Walk*

Returning outside, a gravel path around a square of lawn just west of this end of the Dormitory structure now marks the location of the Cloister Walk. If the High Altar was the spiritual centre of the abbey, this was its logistical centre: the intersection point of much of the traffic moving between the various parts of the complex: the Abbey Church to the north (Stop 8), with the East (Stops 6–7, 10–11), West (Stop 13) and South Ranges (Stop 14) filling out the compass. Though originally

The cloister of Battle Abbey sits in front of what is now the Battle Abbey School. (*Michael Livingston*)

of comparatively simple design, this pathway was remodelled several times during the abbey's lifetime. During its heyday, the walk would have had fine pavement and intricate stone vaulting above, surrounding a central garden where grass now grows.

13 The West Range

Looming over the Cloister Walk is the West Range. Though now greatly expanded and remodelled, this large stone building was originally a storage area for the cellarer, who was in charge of interacting with the laity in trading and in acquiring and maintaining provisions for the abbey. In the thirteenth century, as the riches of Battle Abbey grew, this space was remodelled into lodgings for the abbot, his household and his guests. Further remodelling occurred in the fifteenth century. The combined opulence and ongoing utility of what was then effectively a grand country house ensured its survival even after the suppression that destroyed so much of the rest of the abbey. Today, it serves as the home of the Battle Abbey School and can be visited only during school holidays.

Along the ground floor of the West Range, facing the Cloister Walk, the arches against the wall of the Abbot's Lodging are evidence of the ornate vaulting and stonework that formerly covered what is now gravel paths. From right to left (north to south), the first seven arches date from the fifteenth century; the next two date from the thirteenth century and feature the remains of blind tracery. The windows that are interspersed amid the arches were put in place after the suppression of the abbey.

Through the doors on the northernmost end of the building is the Outer Parlour, beyond which sits the Outer Court (not visible from an exterior tour): this marked the limiting point of interaction between visitors and the monks of the abbey.

Rising behind the Abbot's Lodging is the Abbot's Hall, which dates from the fifteenth century. Like many other parts of the West Range, this hall was ravaged by fire in 1931, though efforts were made to restore much of its appearance.

The southernmost wing of this complex of buildings, which will become more visible as the tour continues, is a Library Wing, built in the nineteenth century.

14 The South Range

The South Range consists of the sites of the abbey's Refectory (immediately south of the Cloister Walk) and Kitchen (south of the Refectory). Among the three windows on the wall of the West Range are the remains of blind tracing that was formerly on the interior of the Refectory.

15 The Guest Range

Returning to the east-west road across the grounds, a walk back towards the Great Gatehouse passes along the nineteenth-century Terrace Walk, which allows multiple viewpoints down along the slope of the traditional battlefield. To the right, north of this walk, are the buttressed undercrofts and two tall towers that are all that remains of the Guest Range. Originally

Buttressed undercrofts and lone towers are all that remain today of the once-impressive Guest Range. (*Michael Livingston*)

built for abbey guests in the thirteenth century, it was rebuilt in more opulent form after the suppression of the abbey before being taken down in the eighteenth century.

Tour Stops Outside the Abbey
Aside from the general charms of the town of Battle, there are within walking distance three immediate points of interest for those seeking the remains of 1066.

16 *St Mary's Parish Church*
It may seem strange that the Battle of Hastings is named for a town 6 miles (9.6km) away, but this reveals an important fact about the site

St Mary's Parish Church, Battle. (*Michael Livingston*)

itself: Harold and William fought upon ground that was essentially in the middle of nowhere in 1066. Hastings, the town from which William had marched, was the closest recognizable location.

The construction of Battle Abbey changed all that. As it was built, labourers would have settled nearby, soon joined by merchants and other comers hoping to gain profit of one kind or another from living within close proximity to the abbey. In the first years, these townsfolk joined the monks for services, but it was soon clear that a better arrangement would be required. These additional churchgoers were too noisy for the austere monks!

As a result, in 1115 the abbey founded St Mary's, a parish church just outside their precinct walls. The church remains in use today, just across High Street at a point that is directly north of the crypts of the monks' Abbey Church. A walk of two minutes from the Great Gatehouse will bring the abbey visitor to its front steps. Inside, visitors can see fourteenth-century wall paintings, a tremendously well-preserved gilded sixteenth-century alabaster tomb and a stained-glass window commemorating the Battle of Hastings.

17 The First Roundabout

Following the A2100 east, a further walk of two to three minutes beyond St Mary's, the visitor will find the First Roundabout where Marley Lane meets High Street. A bench on the northern side of this Roundabout affords a look down the A2100 as it continues south-east toward Hastings. While rather nondescript in comparison to the grand vistas of the Abbey, this location is the best place to visualize what we believe is the most likely reconstruction of the battle.

The A2100 is believed to follow the rough path of the road that William followed up from his encampment – a path along the relatively flat ridgelines, above the often boggy valley bottoms. For the advancing William, the road was not just a conducive means of moving men and material, it was high ground.

Military leaders have long understood the importance of gaining high ground over the enemy. Our sources make clear that Harold achieved just that in 1066: arriving first on the field of battle, he formed his shield-wall on the highest ground possible in order to put his enemy at a disadvantage. On the other side, though put in the position of needing to react, William would have wanted to keep

The First Roundabout, looking down the road up which William's forces would have come. (*Michael Livingston*)

to what high ground he had at hand, as well, in order to minimize that disadvantage.

The traditional retelling of the battle that is featured at Battle Abbey today, however, requires William to have abandoned the high ground of the road in order to move his men *downhill* to form his lines in the boggy valley bottom where ponds now lie (Stop 5 above). No source mentions such a descent. Even stranger, the traditional reconstruction has the English line along the ridge, looking down into the valley, a position that is parallel to the road. If William had instead stayed on the high ground, he would have rolled up the English flank – which would have been absolutely to his advantage. The traditional tactics, to put it simply, make no sense.

More likely, the English set themselves across the road, with their lines wrapping around the ridge to prevent any attempt at a flanking manoeuvre. William rolled his own lines out accordingly, keeping to the high ground and the road as best he could. The crest of the ridge would have been the focal point of his attack and it was there that Harold planted his banner – where Battle Abbey is today.

The result of this would be a roughly 90-degree rotation of the battle, pivoting around the fixed point of the High Altar of the church. William's lines would run more north-south than east-west. Harold's shield-wall would have been a great bow around the summit of the hill. Sitting on the Roundabout bench, the visitor can thus imagine William's men and horses charging up and back along the A2100, with Harold's mighty shield-wall stretching across the street nearby. Interestingly, it was near here, around the top of Marley Lane, that an important axe-head was found in 1951. This artefact can be seen at the Battle Museum of Local History (Stop 18).

Unfortunately, for all the tactical logic that such a scenario presents, it leaves us with a new problem: fitting the necessary men on this spot. We don't know exactly how many men Harold had, but estimates often fall between 7,000 and 10,000. For the sake of argument here, let's assume an even smaller number of 5,000. His shield-wall was tightly packed, which surely can't be any tighter than shoulder-to-shoulder. So how wide was the average man of the fyrd in 1066? A 1988 survey of military personnel in the United States gave a mean breadth of 21.5in (54.61cm) for males. When we add clothing, armour and minimal space to manoeuvre, 2ft (61cm) seems a solid working guess. If we estimate a depth of 10 men in the shield-wall, then our formation of a very conservative number of 5,000 men would need to be 1,000ft (305m) wide at a minimum. Yet the ridge is less than half that width. To achieve the kind of minimal line length we need, we would need to imagine the English not just fronting the hill here, but also wrapping around the side of it to encompass the traditional placement of the lines – facing down the open slopes. This, then, brings us back to the problems already discussed with that scenario!

18 *The Battle Museum of Local History*

A five-minute walk in the opposite direction from the First Roundabout, the Battle Museum of Local History is situated in the Almonry, a charming building along High Street that was originally part of an Elizabethan walled garden. The local collections here house several items of interest to those seeking to understand

Hastings, including replica prints of the Bayeux Tapestry and, most intriguingly, what appears to be the head of a battleaxe that appears to date from the time of the battle. This artefact, found in 1951 near the Roundabout (Stop 17), is one of the only items unearthed anywhere in the area that might connect to the Battle of Hastings. The museum features not just the axe-head itself, but also a full-scale replica of how it might have appeared in 1066.

19 *The Second Roundabout*

Just over 300ft (100m) further up the road from Stop 18 is a Second Roundabout at the junction of the A2100 (High Street) and the A271 (North Trade Road). Stop 17 suggested some reasons to think the battle might need to be partially rotated from the traditional view; this stop marks the only other alternative reconstruction of the battle that could be considered plausible at present.

As we have already stated, there is no reason to doubt the tradition, which dates back to the time of William himself, that Battle Abbey marks the spot where he became the Conqueror. The High Altar of its church is the single best fixed point we have in our search for the Battle of Hastings. But what if it marks the location not of Harold's standard, but *William's*? Such a spot would equally be the place where William won his victory. It would also conceivably fit with the tradition that the spot is specifically where Harold's body lay after the battle: as soon as his corpse was identified, after all, it would have been brought into William's presence.

If this is so, then this Second Roundabout was likely in the thick of the action. The lines would have run to the left and right across this area, backed up onto the ridgeline of Caldbec Hill, which rises to the north here. This provides a significantly higher position than the traditional position on Senlac Hill. Even more suggestive, the terrain here would enable more men to fit across the English front: as we have seen, the position at Senlac is such an effective bottleneck that it's difficult to line up the thousands of men who fought and died here in 1066.

Chapter 6

WILLIAM'S MARCH
TO LONDON

After the battle, the Normans returned to Hastings. William buried his dead, tended to his wounded and plotted his next move. Harold Godwinson, the king of England, was dead. One way or another, as we set out at the beginning of this book, William had his mortal remains quietly disposed of. What would come next, William surely hoped, would be the quick capitulation of the kingdom. It was not to be. Messages sped across the countryside that the king was dead. What came back in return was defiance.

The *witena-gemot* was much diminished after the defeat at Hastings. Harold had been not just king, but also the earl of Wessex. Alongside him had died two of the five other earls of the realm, his brothers Gyrth and Leofwine, who together held most of the lands south of a line across the island from the Severn to the Wash. Earls Morkere and Edwin remained – representing Northumbria and Mercia, respectively, though we don't know at this moment whether they were still in York or had moved south – but whatever their military strength might have been just a month earlier, it had been shattered by the disaster of Fulford Gate. The other remaining earl was Waltheof, who controlled the new (and relatively small) earldom of Northamptonshire and Huntingdonshire. Joining them were the major clergymen of the country, who were led by Stigand, the Archbishop of Canterbury and Ealdred, the Archbishop of York.

We don't know whether these men met in person or simply exchanged messages in the turmoil. But we know their resolve: no one was ready to bend the knee to the Norman duke. Instead, most of them wanted to put forward a new man for the crown: Edgar Atheling, whose grandfather, Edmund Ironside, and great-grandfather, Athelred, and great-great-grandfather, Edgar I, had all been kings of England. However, unlike Harold, who was crowned at once, it seems there was no coronation for Edgar Atheling. This could mean that the young man – he was around 15 at the time – had doubters or doubts of his own or it could simply mean that William's actions moved faster than arrangements could be made.

It's difficult to establish the full sequence of events across the next weeks, but it's at least tempting to suppose that it was news of Edgar Atheling's election that prompted William's next move: he would march out from the safety of the Hastings peninsula and campaign to win his crown.

His destination, as everyone knew it must be, would be London and Westminster. The only question was how to get there. Thanks to William of Poitiers, we have a decent notion of the duke's route, which in turn enables us to recognize something of his thinking behind it. William wouldn't march straight for the capital. Instead, he would make his way around the coastline. It was a patient, safe decision that put him always in reach of the sea. A fleet of some thousand and more ships had brought him to the shores of the kingdom. He probably sent some number of these back to Normandy for reinforcements or resupplies. But at least some would trace the coast parallel to his march, ferrying supplies as they came, while providing a constant means of escape if needed.

With the privilege of hindsight, we can say that he didn't need to worry much about the immediate response. No matter its defiance, the kingdom's military might was largely destroyed. Fulford Gate, Stamford Bridge and now Hastings … how many huscarls still lived is not known, but they could not have been many. Almost the only thing left to throw at the invaders would be the fyrd, the local militias. William probably suspected this, but he nevertheless wanted to move forward with caution. After all, if he'd heard one thing about the fate of Harald Hardrada and Tostig Godwinson, it would be that they had underestimated their enemy's capability to muster and mobilize its army.

Some time after the Battle of Hastings, then, William's army was on the move, leaving behind a contingent to maintain their beachhead. The *Carmen* says it was five days after the battle. Modern historians measure it closer to three weeks. Marching past any corpses of those English who'd not yet been buried, they made their way around Romney Marsh. According to William of Poitiers, the duke's first target was the town of Romney itself, where some of his ships had accidentally come ashore during the initial crossing of the English Channel on the night of 27/28 September. The townspeople had slaughtered the Norman crews and now William 'inflicted such punishment as he saw fit' in vengeance. It was an act that was surely intended both to rally his men and to put the English on warning.

Roman Remnants

Most of us today think of Rome as a deeply distant thing – *ancient* history – but it bears remembering that the Norman Conquest is as close to the building of the Colosseum in Rome as it is to our modern day. For William and his contemporaries Rome wasn't just a cultural memory – it was also still a physical presence on the ground. Roman roads remained the arteries of both commerce and war across much of the former empire. Roman engineering still brought water, cleared sewage and underlay the structures of some of the biggest cities. And even its abandoned magnificence could dominate the landscape. In the poem 'The Ruin', an anonymous poet of early medieval England marvelled at the remnants of a Roman city – likely Bath – that had been empty for centuries:

Wondrous are these wall-stones, wasted by fate,
The courtyards crumpled, giants' works corrupted,
The roofs tumbled down, towers in ruins,
Frozen gate fractured, frost mixed in the mortar,
Scarred storm-roofs raked and scored,
Undone by the years. The earthen grip yokes
Its proud builders, perished, long departed,
The hard grasp of the grave, until a hundred generations
Of people have passed. But this place outlasted,
Gray with lichen, stained red,
Knew one reign after another,
Still stood after storms. The high arch has succumbed,
But the wall-stone still stands in the winds …

Next, the Normans came to Dover, which William of Poitiers describes as being already impressively fortified – though by no means would it have compared to the extraordinary fortifications that exist there today. What it had, for certain, was a hill topped by the earthen rampart of an Iron Age hillfort, in the middle of which the Romans had built a lighthouse that early English settlers re-used as a bell tower for a small church: St Mary de Castro. The natural harbour below the hill had been the site of the Roman town of Dubris, which had a fort to protect a garrison of the *Classis Brittanica* naval force. This fort was replaced in the construction of a Roman Saxon Shore fort in the third century AD.

Whatever the remains of these Roman fortifications – and however they had been modified by the English town that had taken root there – they were substantial enough that people from around the region had sought their protection. Faced with the sight of the approaching army, however, they lost hope for their defence. The gates were opened to the invaders, some number of whom – 'greedy for booty', Poitiers writes – nevertheless set fire to part of the town. The flames were quickly put out and William seems to have made a show of his fury at his men overstepping their orders: he paid the townspeople damages and only his inability to identify the guilty members of his army saved their lives.

The Normans spent eight days at Dover and it is here that we get the first report of dysentery in the army. William of Poitiers comments that this was the result of the men eating 'freshly killed meat' and drinking water – though if so these were only the transport for the real culprit of bacteria or amoeba passed from faecal matter into the food or water supplies due to the unhygienic conditions that resulted from so many men sharing the road and camp.

Canterbury, the great city of the south-east and seat of Archbishop Stigand, sent word that it would join Dover in surrendering, but William did not proceed to its Roman walls directly. Instead, after he left his sick men in Dover – both to recover and to protect it as another port – William made his next camp, according to William of Poitiers, at 'the Broken Tower', about a day's ride away. Here, the duke himself fell extremely ill. Whether this was a furtherance of the dysentery from Dover or an unrelated illness, we cannot

Dysentery

The greatest enemy of premodern soldiers was not opposing soldiers but disease, primarily dysentery. Dysentery was a type of gastroenteritis – that is, bloody diarrhoea. The cause was simple and it would have been simple to avoid, had premodern armies understood that placing latrines and tethering horses too close to water sources would contaminate them with faecal matter. But they didn't, despite the numerous deaths of kings on campaign: Henry the Young King of England in 1183; John of England in 1216; Saint Louis IX of France in 1270; King Edward I of England in 1307; and Henry V of England in 1422. Whole armies could be laid low by the disease. Marching across northern France in 1415, Henry V lost approximately 30 per cent of his army to illness, including more than 50 per cent of his men-at-arms. Many of the archers who brought him victory at Agincourt are said to have done so without pants – the easier to relieve themselves when the urge struck.

Sin – particularly fornication – was the explanation most frequently given for why dysentery hit an army. As the anonymous author of the *Eulogium historiarum* records the reason for the Bishop of Norwich's defeat at the siege of Ypres in 1383: *percussitque eos Deus in posterior* (God hit them in the asses!).

know, but it was clearly a serious and alarming threat to William's health.

If Edgar Atheling had not already been elected king by the English nobles upon hearing word of Harold's death, the news that William had fallen dangerously ill might well have instilled the hope necessary to bring it about. In any event, it was around this time that the monks of Peterborough Abbey asked Edgar to confirm their new abbot – an act that very much assumed his position as the king.

The identity of the 'Broken Tower' where William was stricken has been a matter of some mystery, but it was almost certainly the site near Sandwich now called Richborough Castle. We have already seen how William repeatedly took advantage of existing fortifications in the landscape. Once more, as it had been at both Dover and Pevensey, the place he chose for his encampment was a Roman Saxon Shore fort.

We know William had taken Pevensey, Hastings, Romney and Dover. To these we can almost assuredly add Winchelsea, Rye, Hythe and Lympne, which were also along his route. Adding Richborough and Sandwich would mean that the Normans had seized every major seaport in Kent, giving them an enormous advantage in protecting supplies and reinforcements that might need to be shipped across the English Channel.

As it was at Pevensey, the coastline at Richborough today is far different than it was in William's day. Richborough previously stood at the edge of the sea: a strait, called Wantsum Channel, ran from the English Channel at Sandwich to the Thames Estuary at Reculver, separating the Isle of Thanet (today the tip of Kent) from the rest of England. Over time, shifting shingles at the channel's mouth and the silting of the River Stour at its centre, joined Thanet to the mainland. The Romans, recognizing the strait's importance as a shipping route with excellent harbours, had protected it with forts at both ends: at Richborough (Latin Rutupiae) in the south and at Reculver (Regulbium) in the north.

Though off the beaten track today, Richborough was especially prosperous during the Roman period. The Romans had first come to the island in 55 and 54 BC under the command of Julius Caesar, but a successful attempt at conquest didn't occur until AD 43, when Emperor Claudius sent four legions across the English Channel. If they didn't first come ashore at Richborough – many think they did – then they certainly established a port there soon enough afterwards: archaeologists have found remnants of mid-first century Roman works on the site.

As the Romans spread inland, they built roads to move troops and material across the countryside. The more well-travelled the route, the wider and more well-developed the road – and no Roman road in Britain was more travelled and more recognized for its importance than Watling Street, which ran from the port at Richborough to Canterbury, then cut north-west through London to Wroxeter. When England was Britannia, this was its most major thoroughfare. For a quarter of a millennium, then, Richborough was the gateway to the island.

It was almost assuredly for this reason that the Romans built a magnificent triumphal arch at Richborough – the only one known in

England – around the same time that they proclaimed their conquest of the island complete in AD 83 or 84. The arch stood a staggering 80ft (24m) high, making it one of the largest such monuments in the whole of the Roman Empire. The tower was robbed of much of its stone when the site was converted into the impressively walled Saxon Shore fort that dominates the landscape today, but something of its height might well have remained in use as a watchtower even into 1066. Not only would the physical remains and residual memory of this massive structure fit with William of Poitiers' description of the Normans staying at a 'Broken Tower', but Richborough also fits with what we know of the Conqueror's location (one day north from Dover), his modus operandi (re-using existing fortifications) and his logistical plans (maintaining contact with the sea).

William of Poitiers says that William, despite his weakness, didn't tarry long here and from the *Carmen* we learn that he now moved his forces the short distance to Canterbury, where his illness forced him to remain for a longer time.

Though he was personally ill, he must have known that every day he delayed in the south-east was a day more for his enemies to gather any strength that they might be attempting to rally in London. He knew, too, that every day he remained in the field was one more day he had to supply his army – no small task in a foreign land. William of Poitiers certainly speaks to this latter concern when he tells us that the Conqueror was specifically concerned for his supplies during this period. For many reasons, then, William needed to know if he could seize London directly.

Here, then, was the final reason to encamp at Richborough and then Canterbury: William was now astride Watling Street, which had certainly not disappeared when the Romans left. Such was the awareness of this road that when King Alfred the Great signed his famous treaty with King Guthrum of the Danes, it was Watling Street that formed a key part of the boundary between their spheres of influence. For William, Watling Street was an open road straight into the heart of London.

The Four Highways

During the reign of King Stephen (r. 1135–54), a collection of law codes appeared that claimed to be a record of the English legal system at the time of the Norman Conquest, as told to William the Conqueror in 1070 by 'English nobles who were wise men and learned in their law'. Called the *Laws of Edward the Confessor*, it was a fake. Following in the footsteps of William's own propagandists, like William of Poitiers, its twelfth-century author was working to minimize the traumas of the Conquest – and thus further legitimize it – by presenting old English laws as almost entirely in line with their Norman replacements.

Among its claims is that there were four major roads in England – Watling Street (Richborough to London to Wroxeter), Ermine Street (London to Lincoln to York), Fosse Way (Exeter to Cirencester to Lincoln) and Icknield Street (Bourton on the Water to Templeborough) – that had been constructed by the English kings and that royal protection was given to travellers upon them. In point of fact, of course, the roads as they would have lain on the ground were Roman in origin (albeit following ancient trackways in parts) and there was never royal protection of this kind. Despite such falsehoods, however, the *Laws of Edward the Confessor* nevertheless present us with the clear evidence of how important these Roman roads remained well into the Middle Ages: many call them the Four Highways of medieval England!

Watling Street underlies much of the A2 today as it passes through Canterbury and Rochester on its way to London. Just south of the Thames, near what is now the London Underground's Borough Station, it was joined by the Roman road to Chichester, called Stane Street (its route largely followed today by the A3, A24, A29 and A285). Watling Street here turned north, crossing the great river at London Bridge before passing through the city and continuing north-west into the country.

William of Poitiers reports that William, as we would expect, took advantage of the speed afforded by the Roman-built road to test London's resolve. The taking of Rochester on the way isn't mentioned, though it likely was among the unspecified other towns in the area that we are told surrendered. Certainly the Normans would not have left it in English control when forces could use it to cut his supply lines.

William's forces encountered significant resistance at London Bridge and it was at this time that they set fire to homes in what is now Southwark – perhaps out of anger, perhaps in a failed attempt to draw out whatever was left of the English army in the city.

London's walls would have been a formidable obstacle, but the Thames itself was the bigger problem: if the city wasn't going to open its gates to the Normans, the invaders would be hard pressed to force them either across the bottleneck of London Bridge or by attempting some kind of ship-based assault on the city. If he was going to enter the city, William now knew he'd have to literally take the long way around to get there: he needed to get on the other side of the Thames and approach London from the north.

The only question would have been how to do so: he could march his army around to the north side of the city or he could sail them there. He'd already made a successful landing operation or two at Pevensey and Hastings, of course, but that had been far to the south and completely unopposed. A water-crossing at the Thames Estuary, in contrast, would surely have to contend with the English fleet on the waves even before it had to make an assault on shorelines that were within striking distance of London.

Though historians often give it short shrift, it may be that what William therefore decided was the biggest gamble in a campaign that had already seen its fair share of bold bets and lucky throws: he left the sea behind and marched west, aiming to cross the Thames upriver.

Up to this point, the sea was both a supply line and a safety line. After this point, his army would be forced to maintain logistics entirely upon what they carried with them or could seize from foreign territory. This was a far more difficult endeavour, as it required an army to spread out for foraging at the very time when it most needed to remain cohesive in case it faced attack.

Our sources tell us precious little about the route they took. According to William of Poitiers, the invaders received reinforcements from 'over the sea' around this time – though he doesn't specify where or when or how many. The *Carmen* reports that a detachment of Normans reached Winchester, the royal seat of England since Alfred's

The Domesday Book

In 1086, twenty years after his Conquest, King William the Conqueror's officials completed a survey of the property values of his realm in order to establish taxes. It was an enormous project, in which his assessors sought to ascertain, if possible, the ownership and value of properties at three dates: on the eve of the Conquest, at the time the current tenants received it and at the time of the survey. The assessors' findings are held in a manuscript that came to be called the Domesday Book.

For some 200 years, scholars have attempted to use the data in the Domesday Book to chart the course of William's march through England: if property values declined in the years immediately following the Conquest, it was reckoned, then the loss could be attributable to ravaging on the part of his army.

Unfortunately, there is no consistent pattern in property devaluation that can reveal a path. Among the many problems with such efforts is that while William's men no doubt would have stripped what they could where they could, they would have done so in an inconsistent manner: armies don't forage in a regular pattern, but instead do it unpredictably depending on factors ranging from need and availability to geography and speed of march. Any destruction along the route would have been uneven at the outset. Additionally, property values would have recovered at an inevitably variable rate in the intervening decades – or even declined for completely unrelated reasons due to local calamity. Some property damages might also be attributable to the movements of Harold Godwinson's army or other English forces taking advantage of the chaos of the Conquest. And as if *that* weren't enough, we face the challenge of wondering how accurate the Domesday Book really is. One of the only things as old as taxes, after all, are efforts to avoid them!

time, and there negotiated a deal with the widowed queen of Edward the Confessor: she could keep her dower lands and live as the queen dowager … she just needed not to get in the way. William said he would not go there. Winchester would be spared.

The next place-name we get is from William of Poitiers, who says that the duke crossed the Thames by a ford and bridge at Wallingford, which is some 50 miles (80km) west of Southwark as the crow flies

– and significantly farther by the major roads. Our best guess for his route, in fact, depends on the roads that he needed to take to make speed.

There were the Roman roads, of course. Watling Street had taken him to the south bank of the Thames. From this point there were two major roads heading south-west. There was Stane Street, but for all that this would take him west, it would take him even further south towards Chichester, near the Isle of Wight. This was not the direction he wanted to go.

More possibly, the Normans chose the other road, which ran from London to Winchester: the main route between England's new and old capitals. This was definitely a dominant road through the country in later years: it, not Stane Street, is recorded on the earliest map to show medieval roads in England, a fourteenth-century manuscript called the Gough Map, which is now held by the Bodleian Library in Oxford. It has long been suspected that there was a Roman road underlying this route, which is generally followed by the A3 and A31 today, passing through Kingston-upon-Thames, Guildford, Farnham, Alton and Alresford before reaching Winchester; recent archaeological discoveries appear to have confirmed the ancient road's existence. It was, at any rate, there in 1066. Part of its old track passes along a ridge between Farnham and Guildhall that is today called the Hog's Back. It was here, in 1035, that Edward the Confessor's brother, Alfred, was seized by the men of King Harald Harefoot – despite assurances of safety from Earl Godwin. Not only did this run in a more westerly direction than Stane Street, but it fits with the exchange of messages between William and Edith: his agreement not to lay waste to Winchester best makes sense if he was marching towards it.

Once that agreement was reached, of course, William's entire focus would have been on crossing the Thames. The Gough Map doesn't show the secondary roads that would have branched off from the old Winchester road, but judging from the towns that it shows, we can reckon that there were significant paths running north through Bagshot and/or Basingstoke toward Reading. There was a crossing of the river there, but the Gough Map also shows a major road running past Wallingford on its way to Oxford.

Why William crossed at Wallingford instead of Reading (or any other crossing, for that matter) may be due to the fact that he was met there by Stigand, the Archbishop of Canterbury, who submitted to him.

Who Crowned Harold?

Stigand is a central and fascinating figure in this period. He was made bishop of Winchester in 1047 and in 1052 he was raised to the archdiocese of Canterbury – though he did not give up the rich seat of Winchester. As a result, he was excommunicated by Pope Leo IX (r. 1049–54), as well as his four successors: Victor II (r. 1055–7), Stephen IX (r. 1057–8), Nicholas II (r. 1059–61) and Alexander II (r. 1061–73). Despite this rebuke, he served as a chaplain and advisor to every king of England since Cnut and the power and income he continued to derive from holding the two major benefices was significant. As 1066 began, he and Harold Godwinson were likely the two richest men in the realm.

According to contemporary Norman writers, it was Stigand who crowned Harold king in 1066. According to contemporary English writers, it was Ealdred, the Archbishop of York. The Bayeux Tapestry splits the difference: Stigand is present at Harold's coronation, but he isn't shown crowning him as king. So who did it?

By tradition, the Archbishop of Canterbury crowned the king, but Stigand had personally run afoul of the Pope. This is likely the reason that Norman writers said he performed the rite … though in truth it was almost assuredly Ealdred. Norman propagandists would very much have wanted to suggest that Harold's coronation had been made king by an excommunicated man. No matter what righteousness William felt he had in his cause, the deposition of a rightfully crowned king could have been perceived as troubling. If Harold wasn't properly crowned, then removing him from the throne was a just act indeed!

Stigand had supported Harold as king – he was apparently one of those present for Edward the Confessor's deathbed pronouncement – but when Canterbury had quickly and willingly submitted to William after the Battle of Hastings the duke might have thought the archbishop would support his own claim to the throne. This may be why records from the Domesday Book show that Stigand's personal holdings in Kent don't note much damage from the time of the Conquest.

But Stigand was certainly not of this mind. Instead, every indication we have is that he was among those supporting Edgar Atheling for the crown. The fact that Edgar doesn't appear to have been crowned despite his apparent election, however, speaks to early and worsening cracks in English unity. The brothers Edwin and Morkere, the earls of Mercia and Northumbria, said that they would support Edgar, too, but they soon appear to have wavered – perhaps they had their own desires for the crown now that the rival Godwins were gone or perhaps they had taken stock of their chances against William and begun to despair. In any event, just at the moment when they ought to have been leading a military defence against William, we are told that they took what was left of their forces and withdrew north.

Where the two powerful earls went we don't know, though the English chronicler John of Worcester says they sent their sister, Harold's widow, Ealdgyth, to Chester. We can surmise, therefore, that they themselves had taken to Watling Street, headed in the same direction.

Stigand may have read the writing on the wall at that point – prompted in such literacy, perhaps, by what appears to have been significant damage to his personal holdings in Mortlake, which is just off the road we believe William took out of London. If this destruction, recorded in the Domesday Book, is indeed tied to the Conquest, then it seems William had figured out that the Archbishop wasn't supporting him after all. Stigand's properties were newly in danger and his life might have been, as well. He had still more holdings in Harwell, just 8 miles (12.8km) from Wallingford. With the Normans in the area – perhaps at the very moment heading for the crossings of the Thames at Reading – Stigand's might have seen it as the time to act: he would have sent word to William to meet at Wallingford, where the Conqueror could cross the river and the Archbishop could submit.

After the crossing of the Thames, the next point that our sources give us is Berkhamsted, where we are told that Archbishop Ealdred of York, Earls Edwin and Morkere, Edgar Atheling, the bishops Wulfstan of Worcester and Walter of Hereford, along with chief citizens of London, all submitted to William. The author of the *Anglo-Saxon Chronicle* (D) writes that 'they submitted from necessity when the most harm was done – and it was great folly that it was not done thus earlier'.

Why they all met at Berkhamsted and how the Norman army got there from Wallingford, is uncertain. The Gough Map shows the old road between London and Oxford, part of which followed by today's A40, as a major route. From Wallingford, a march north of only a dozen or so miles along smaller roads was needed to reach it at Tetsworth. It seems fair to assume something like this had been William's aim before he heard that the rest of the English leadership – including the young man who'd been so recently elected king in his place – were willing to submit to his authority. If the earls, perhaps with the others, were on Watling Street, it could be that William marched a further dozen miles north to reach Aylesbury. Here he would have linked up with the old Roman road called Akeman Street, which joined up with Watling Street just north of St Albans. Marching east on this solid road, the Normans would have met the English coming west: Berkhamsted didn't have any great claims to fame prior to 1066, but it *did* happen to sit on Akeman Street, about halfway between Aylesbury and St Albans.

It was early December. The Normans would still face scattered resistance on their way into the capital, if we believe the report of William of Jumièges. The *Carmen* makes reference to preparations being made for a siege of the city at some point, but we have no evidence that there was coordinated resistance between Berkhamsted and London. Though violence would continue, on and off, for years, the war was effectively over.

At the beginning of the month, William entered London as its conqueror. On Christmas Day, he became its king. William of Poitiers indicates that there was debate about how quickly this coronation should take place – William may have wanted to wait for the arrival of his queen-to-be, Matilda, in order to show their joint authority – but the voices urging an earlier ceremony won out. That many of these voices, as William of Poitiers suggests, were English should not surprise us: it might well have been thought that

William's coronation would more quickly put an end to reprisals against the English: the king, after all, ought to have the interests of *all* his people in mind.

As Ealdred, the Archbishop of York, placed the crown on William's head in Westminster Abbey – the church Edward the Confessor had built and where he'd died in January – none could have imagined how much of an impact the Norman Conquest would have. The social and political upheaval would already be in motion and clear to see, of course: twenty years after the Conquest, almost the whole of the upper swath of the landholders in England was Norman; thirty years after the Conquest, not a single English bishopric was in the hands of an Englishman. But so much else changed that could not have been expected.

For instance, the Norman Conquest irrevocably changed the English language. Norman rule – and, with it, Norman rules – brought a need to speak Norman French in order to business with the court and its courts. Over time, French pronunciations bled into non-French words and the Old English of Alfred the Great became the Middle English of Geoffrey Chaucer. From Shakespeare's magnificence to this modest book in your hands, the flexibility of the English language – and all its inconsistencies and incongruities – are a direct result of the coming together of French and English in the years after Hastings.

On a political level, 1066 would ultimately put England on the map of more international interests. Before the Conquest, England was on the outer limits of European notice. After the Conquest, the king of England was also the duke of Normandy – a man with feet on both sides of the English Channel. This would, in coming centuries, bring about the Hundred Years War and so much else that set the stages for England's power stretching its reach (or attempting to do so) across the globe.

TOUR FIVE: WILLIAM'S MARCH

Any effort to account for everything there is to see along the stretch of William's march to London would be counted in books, not in the few pages that we have here. One of the great joys of touring is that history is everywhere. What follows, then, is only the highlights of a select number of locations as they relate to the immediate aftermath of the Battle of Hastings.

Bodiam

Open fields beside the River Rother, immediately south of Bodiam Bridge, mark the location of a Roman town that was likely associated with the surrounding Weald, the iron-working industrial heartland of Roman Britain (and later). From here, a Roman road ran north via Sandhurst to Rochester and south into the forests of the Weald toward Hastings. Importantly, until the late-medieval period the river was navigable from here to the sea, with the result that Bodiam served as an important port for points inland – including, after its founding, Battle Abbey. For Harold's army, Bodiam's Roman road and river crossing (whether then a bridge or ford, we don't know) make it a potential avenue for their march south towards the Hastings peninsula in 1066. By these same measures, Bodiam would have seen the passing of Norman troops a few weeks later.

Since the end of the fourteenth century, the dominant feature of the landscape in the valley has been Bodiam Castle. This stunningly picturesque castle, situated on a moated island, has long drawn visitors. In 1975, footage of it was used for exterior shots of the 'Swamp Castle' in *Monty Python and the Holy Grail*. The site is today held by the National Trust and open for tours (fee required). Visitors should note the gunports near the entrance to the castle, some of the earliest in England, suggesting that the lords of the southern coast continued to worry about invasion into the fifteenth century. It is also in the moat at Bodiam that the so-called Bodiam Mortar was dredged up in the eighteenth century, one of the finest examples of wrought-iron gunpowder weapons in England and now part of the Royal Artillery Museum's collection.

Bodiam Castle. (*Kelly DeVries*)

Lympne

Rising above the flat plains of Romney Marsh – which in 1066 would still have been an arm of the sea – Lympne was a major Roman port (Portus Lemanis). From here, a Roman road called Stone Street ran to Canterbury, where it joined Watling Street. Later, it became the location of a Saxon Shore fort. The much-weathered ruins of this fortification, locally called Stutfall Castle, are on private land. Part of the curtain wall can be viewed from the footpath along Royal Military Road, about 0.5 miles (0.75km) west of the public car park on West Hythe Road. Lympne Castle crests the ridge above the ruins. Begun in the twelfth century, it is privately owned and much changed today.

Dover

Dover boasts an extraordinary history – not surprising given that its natural harbour happens to sit at the closest point to continental Europe. In 55 BC, Julius Caesar attempted to make Dover his initial beachhead from which to conquer Britannia, but he was turned back by the sight of angry, armed Britons massed on the famed White Cliffs. In time, a Roman port would indeed be built here, called Portus Dubris.

The Roman port and a third-century Saxon Shore fort re-using its stones are largely buried under Dover, though parts of both can be seen by visiting the Roman Painted House, often called 'Britain's Pompeii'. Rather than being buried by a volcanic eruption, however, this *mansio* (a hostel for Roman officials) was buried (and thus preserved) by the Romans themselves when they built the Saxon Shore fort atop it. Excavated in the 1970s, the walls of the *mansio* have over 400 square feet of painted plaster – the most found at any site north of the Alps. Visitation times can be irregular and a small entrance fee is required to enter the site (25 New St, Dover CT17 9AJ, UK).

Any trip to Dover must include a visit to Dover Castle, with its history stretching from the Iron Age hill fort at its summit to the tunnels beneath it where British commanders oversaw the Dunkirk evacuation (Operation Dynamo) in 1940. Those following the footsteps of the Conqueror in 1066 should take special note of the small church of St Mary de Castro within its walls, which stood in William's time. William's army spent more than a week in this area, riddled with dysentery and we can be certain that the Conqueror himself visited the promontory. In fact, William of Poitiers describes the Normans 'adding new fortifications' to the castle they found here: part of these formed a ring around the church and tower that in the thirteenth century were replaced with the earthen bank and stone wall that visitors climb today. It was around this same time that the Roman lighthouse beside the church – one of two Roman lighthouses that had framed Dover's harbour (its western counterpart is gone) – was converted from a guardroom to a bell tower for the congregation.

Of course, whatever the Normans found on the site – and no matter what they added to it – Dover Castle would have looked nothing like

The enormous size of Dover Castle is apparent from any direction, but a view from the air makes clear just how formidable the fortifications are that have built up around the keep at its heart.

The church within the walls of Dover Castle, with the former Roman lighthouse beside it. (*Kelly DeVries*)

the massive complex it is today, the largest castle in England. Dover Castle as it stands now took shape largely during the reign of King Henry II (r. 1154–89). The Great Keep has been renovated to appear much as it did in the medieval period. There are fees to enter the site, which is now administered by English Heritage.

Richborough

The likely location for the 'Broken Tower' that William visited after leaving Dover is today maintained by English Heritage as the Richborough Roman Fort and Amphitheatre (Richborough Rd, Sandwich CT13 9JW, UK; a small fee required for admission). The massive walls of the Saxon Shore fort dominate the site – every bit as impressive as those on view at Pevensey. The grounds also show much evidence of the original Roman port of Rutupiae, including shops, granaries, a *mansio* and the remains of the triumphal arch that was built here to mark the 'official' entrance to Roman Britannia. A gravel rectangle shows the outlines of this monumental structure's foundations, which run some 33ft (10m) deep into the ground. Atop this, the cross-shaped platform today is what is left of the raised walkways beneath the four arches of the monument: a symbol of the crossroads that the town itself represented. To the east hummed the sea-harbour on the Wantsum Channel (now silted in). To the west ran the great Roman road of Watling Street, extending from the gate ahead to Canterbury and then on to London.

This arch would have towered over 80ft (24m) above the Roman city: roughly the height of a modern eight-storey building and an absolutely daunting sight in the landscape when it was built around AD 85. The monument was clad in white marble from the famed quarries of Carrara in northern Tuscany, which was further embellished with sculptures and inscriptions in both marble and bronze. From its top, a keen-eyed observer could have seen ships approaching when they were only halfway across the English Channel and at least a portion of the structure is believed to have continued in use as a watchtower even after it was robbed of much of its stone in later centuries to build the Saxon Shore fort and other nearby structures. It is the memory of this service that probably lies behind William of Poitiers' identification of the site with a 'Broken Tower'.

A look across Richborough shows the impressive size of the Roman fort. In the middle left, with two men standing atop it, is the four-armed foundation of the tower that once dominated the site. (*Michael Livingston*)

Canterbury

The great number of medieval remains – and the cultural and historical importance of those remains – makes Canterbury one of the great jewels of England. The sites are mostly clustered around the city centre and can be approached in any order and any direction.

Canterbury was an important Roman town and later centre for the people of Kent, but its central place in English history is tied to the arrival in AD 597 of the future Saint Augustine on his mission to spread Christianity. After Augustine made early converts in Kent, the realm's king allowed him to found an abbey in Canterbury,

The pitted face of Richborough's Roman walls is due to the robbing of its facing stones over the centuries. (*Kelly DeVries*)

which quickly became a major Christian centre and remained so throughout the Middle Ages. Though Saint Augustine's Abbey was dismantled following the Dissolution of the Monasteries by Henry VIII, the ruins are today preserved by English Heritage and can be toured for a small fee.

Ruins of the church at Canterbury Abbey. (*Michael Livingston*)

Looming over the site of Saint Augustine's Abbey is Canterbury Cathedral, which was founded in 597 but completely rebuilt and expanded in the years immediately after the Norman Conquest. Even more modifications and extensions occurred after the 1170 murder here of Thomas à Becket made him a saint – and the small cathedral chapel at which he was martyred one of the most visited pilgrimage sites in medieval Christendom. Today, the cathedral is a heavily visited World Heritage Site (entrance fee required). Beyond the extraordinary glory of the cathedral itself, visitors should be sure to take special note of Becket's shrine and the tombs of Edward the Black Prince (d. 1376) and King Henry IV (d. 1413).

Canterbury was walled by the Romans around AD 300, though the walls visible today date to the fourteenth century. The best view of these is at the Westgate, beside the junction of the A290 and A2050. The gatehouse through which it passes is 60ft (18m) in height, the tallest surviving medieval gatehouse in England. The

Canterbury Cathedral. (*Kelly DeVries*)

A2050 probably marks the line of Watling Street as it starts its course toward Rochester and then London, meaning that this gatehouse, built in 1380, would have been that which the pilgrims in Chaucer's famed *Canterbury Tales* can be imagined to have passed through on their way to Becket's shrine.

Rochester
Though not specifically mentioned among the stops made by the Conqueror, we can be assured that Rochester would have surrendered to him before he moved on toward London: sited between the River Medway and the sea, on Watling Street between Canterbury and the

The Cloister Walk of Canterbury Cathedral. Archbishop Thomas Becket was martyred just inside the doorway at the far end of this walkway, along which his murderers would have approached. (*Michael Livingston*)

The Westgate of Canterbury. (*Michael Livingston*)

capital, the city was too strategically important to leave uncontrolled. Indeed, Rochester's importance is signalled by the fact that Bishop Odo was given control of it after the Conquest. The bishop built an initial castle here, which was replaced by a stone castle between 1087 and 1089. This lies at the heart of the stone keep that is the castle's most prominent feature today: an imposing stone structure much expanded in the twelfth century. Administered by English Heritage, it is open to the public (fees required).

The impressive keep of Rochester Castle today.

Wallingford

A visit to Wallingford today should begin at the local museum (Flint House, 52 High St, Wallingford OX10 0DB, UK). Aside from its display of a few artefacts, the museum sits on High Street, which lies atop the main road leading to the bridge over the Thames on the east side of town. Across the street from the museum is Kinecroft Park; visible around its western and southern edges are mounded ridges that remain from the early English fortifications. By the time the Normans arrived in Wallingford, these earthen walls would have been topped with a wooden palisade above a moat.

This earthen rampart is the remains of the original fortifications of Wallingford that William would have seen when he arrived here in 1066. (*Kelly DeVries*)

The bridge over the River Thames at Wallingford today. The ford crossed by William would have been near this spot. (*Michael Livingston*)

Surely recognizing the importance of the Thames crossing here after using it himself in 1066, William ordered the building of a new fortification to protect the area. Wallingford Castle would grow to become an impressive complex along the river – too impressive, Oliver Cromwell thought, as he tore it down in 1652. What remains today is a motte, part of a moat, a few fragments of walls and a memory of grandeur. These remains sit in the north-east corner of town, beside the Thames, within Wallingford Castle Meadows (Wallingford, OX10 8LG, UK). Visiting is free during the day, with access through gates on Cemetery Lane, the Thames Path or Castle Lane.

Little remains of Wallingford Castle, though impressive views can still be had from its heavily wooded motte. (*Kelly DeVries*)

Berkhamsted

It was at Berkhamsted, as we saw above, that William received the submission of the would-be king Edgar Atheling, the earls Morkere and Edwin and so many other leading men of the realm. The town was then likely closer to Northchurch, situated along the Roman road called Akeman Street. After the Conquest, William directed his half-brother, Robert of Mortain, to construct a fortification to impose Norman control on the area. A short way from the English settlement, he built Berkhamsted Castle (White Hill, Berkhamsted HP4 1LJ, UK), a motte-and-bailey that is now under the control of English Heritage. The town, over time, gravitated toward it to take the position it has today.

Berkhamsted Castle today. (*Anne Thorniley*)

Westminster

In many respects the story of 1066 begins and ends at Westminster Abbey (entrance fee required), where Edward the Confessor died and both Harold Godwinson and William the Conqueror were crowned. The Confessor's tomb is here, along with those of many other kings and queens of England – not to mention Chaucer and so many other figures of English history. For this reason alone it is worth a visit. As mentioned in Chapter 1, the Pyx Chamber and undercroft are the only remains of Edward's abbey visible today.

Close beside the abbey is the Palace of Westminster, the oldest part of which is Westminster Hall. This great hall was built in 1097 by William the Conqueror's son, William II Rufus, and it was then the largest such hall in Europe. Visiting requires passage through security and other restrictions depending on sessions of Parliament or other times of increased security.

Westminster Abbey holds the tombs of many of England's kings and queens – and a great many tourists. (*Michael Livingston*)

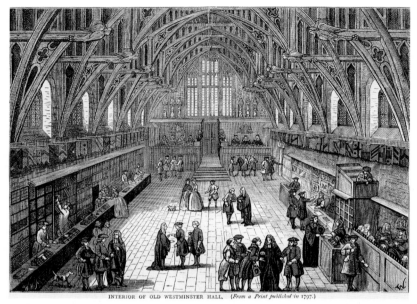

INTERIOR OF OLD WESTMINSTER HALL. (*From a Print published in* 1797.)

An 1810 engraving, showing the interior of Westminster Hall as it then appeared. (Thomas Rowlandson (1756–1827) and Augustus Charles Pugin (1762–1832) (after) John Bluck (fl. 1791–1819), Joseph Constantine Stadler (fl. 1780–1812), Thomas Sutherland (1785–1838), J. Hill, and Harraden (*aquatint engravers*))

London

Moving east from Westminster, the one city melting into the other, we come to London. The sites to be seen here are simply too numerous to list and must include the city's great cultural touchstones like the British Library, the British Museum and the Museum of London. There is space for only a few other highlights.

The London Bridge that in William's day had been the primary crossing of the Thames – and had been since the Romans first built one on the site more than a millennium earlier – is gone. The bridge on the site now was built in 1973, replacing a bridge built in 1831 that was dismantled and moved to Lake Havasu City in the United States. Before that, there was a stone bridge that had lasted more than six centuries. Completed in 1209, construction on this span

My Fair Lady

London Bridge is the subject of one of the most well-known English nursery rhymes:

London Bridge is falling down,
Falling down, falling down,
London Bridge is falling down,
My fair lady!

Intriguingly, no one really knows if the rhyme is referring to a specific moment. The medieval London Bridge was seemingly in a state of needing continuous repairs, so almost any time in its history would fit.

As for the 'fair lady', no one know who she is, either. Some think it's a reference to any number of figures of royalty, while others consider it a reference to the Virgin Mary. Another possibility is that she is the nearby tributary the River Lea!

began in 1176 under the order of King Henry II, who viewed it as a penitential act for the murder of Thomas à Becket: a chapel built to honour Becket, which sat at the mid-point of the bridge, marked the traditional beginning of the pilgrimage down Watling Street to Canterbury. Before Henry's stone bridge there was a succession of wooden bridges back to the first Roman crossing around AD 50. All these earlier bridges crossed the Thames about 100ft (30m) west of the current bridge. The south end of the old location would have come out directly beside Southwark Cathedral (St Saviour and St Mary Overie); the north end was beside the church of St Magnus the Martyr.

'View of London Bridge,' by Claude de Jongh (1632). Note the chapel near the centre span: this was dedicated to Saint Thomas à Becket and was the traditional starting point for the pilgrimage to Canterbury. (*Yale Center for British Art, Paul Mellon Fund*)

The Tower of London is today a major tourist attraction and holds the Crown Jewels. (*Michael Livingston*)

The remains of the Roman walls of Londinium can be seen in various parts of the old city of London, but one of the best places to see them is beside Tower Hill Garden, just outside the Tower Hill Tube station. The first 13ft (4m) of the visible wall date from the Roman period; the rest of its height, which extends up to a total of some 33ft (10m), dates from the medieval period. The original Roman walls would have been about 20ft (6m) high.

Close beside Tower Hill stands one of the most iconic sites in all of England: the Tower of London, construction on which was begun almost as soon as William the Conqueror seized the city. His first fortification was made of wood, surrounded with a palisade and ditches, but already he had plans to build a great central keep out of stone that would serve as both a royal refuge and symbol. Around 1078, work on this massive building began. It would come to be called the White Tower. Initial construction was completed enough for William to stay there before his death in 1087. Prior to this point, he often stayed in Barking Abbey; the few ruins of this that remain today are in a park called Abbey Green in Barking, across the street from the thirteenth-century St Margaret's Church (15 North Street, Barking IG11, UK). The first White Tower, as it happens, was not white: the decision to whitewash the stone was made by King Henry III in 1240; it was also this king who greatly expanded much of the keep and the surrounding complex of walls and other fortifications. Today, the Tower of London houses excellent displays from the Royal Armouries, wonderful guides to the working of the medieval castle and, of course, the Crown Jewels.

There is no more fitting end to a tour of 1066 than the Tower of London. So many of the stops on our post-Hastings tour have featured castles or other fortifications and this is no coincidence: for the English, the years after 1066 saw the Normans enforcing their control on the people by imposing their military might upon the landscape. Today's romantic vistas would then have been terrorizing symbols of authoritarian power as they rose across England's landscape.

The moat and walls of the Tower of London, with Tower Bridge in the distance and the White Tower at far right. (*Michael Livingston*)

FURTHER READING

Histories of the Battle of Hastings were written almost from the moment it ended, but in the interest of a shorter recommended reading list, our sense is that modern historical studies start with Edward August Freeman's six-volume *The History of the Norman Conquest of England* (published by Oxford University Clarendon Press between 1867 and 1879). Although dated, it still holds great value.

Freeman's torch was picked up by another master historian, Sir Frank M. Stenton. Stenton's most famous work is his volume in the Oxford History of England, *Anglo Saxon England* (3rd ed., Oxford: Clarendon Press, 1971) at the end of which he summarizes the Norman Conquest and its immediate aftermath. He also wrote *William the Conqueror and the Rule of the Normans* (New York and London: G.P. Putnam's Sons, 1908), and his edition and study on *The Bayeux Tapestry* (London: Phaidon Press, 1957) is still one of the best books on this very important source of the battle.

A legion of studies have followed the lead of Freeman and Stenton. While most focus on the Battle of Hastings, many also delve into the history of William the Conqueror, the initiation of his conquest and his post-conquest rule. They all vary in some interpretations, but none so far have been judged 'the best', so no doubt many similar studies are likely to appear in the upcoming years. Among these are: R. Allen Brown, *The Normans and the Norman Conquest* (2nd ed., Woodbridge: The Boydell Press, 1985); Jim Bradbury, *The Battle of Hastings* (Stroud: Sutton Publishing, 1998); Matthew Bennett, *Campaigns of the Norman Conquest* (London: Osprey, 2001); M.K. Lawson, *The Battle of Hastings, 1066* (Stroud: Tempus, 2002); Richard Huscroft, *The Norman Conquest: An Introduction* (Harlow: Pearson Longman, 2009); and the articles collected in David Bates (ed.), *1066 in Perspective* (Leeds: Royal Armouries Museum, 2018).

On the battle alone, Stephen Morillo's 'Hastings: An Unusual Battle', is important. It appeared originally in the *Haskins Society Journal* 2 (1990), pp. 96–103, but it has been reprinted in numerous places including Matthew Strickland (ed.), *Anglo-Norman Warfare: Studies in Late Anglo-Saxon and Anglo-Norman Military Organization and Warfare* (Woodbridge: The Boydell Press, 1992); and John France (ed.), *Medieval Warfare, 1000-1300* (Aldershot: Ashgate, 2006).

Biographies of the main actors are also of interest in studying the Conquest and battle. William, the duke of Normandy, is particularly well served by Stenton's biography mentioned above; Frank Barlow, *William I and the Norman Conquest* (New York: Collier Books, 1965); David C. Douglas, *William the Conqueror* (Berkeley and Los Angeles: University of California Press, 1964); and David Bates, *William the Conqueror* (New Haven: Yale University Press, 2016). Edward the Confessor is the subject of Barlow's *Edward the Confessor* (Berkeley and Los Angeles: University of California Press, 1970). Also essential on William is John Gillingham's 'William the Bastard at War', in C. Harper-Bill et al. (eds), *Studies in Medieval History Presented to R. Allen Brown* (Woodbridge: Boydell Press, 1989), which was reprinted in *Anglo-Norman Warfare*. The Godwin family has two excellent biographies: Frank Barlow, *The Godwins: The Rise and Fall of a Noble Dynasty* (Harlow: Longman, 2002); and Emma Mason, *The House of Godwine: The History of a Dynasty* (London: Hambledon, 2004). Harold Godwinson has one: Ian W. Walker, *Harold: The Last Anglo-Saxon King* (Stroud: Sutton Publishing, 1997). Harald Hardrada's story can be found in the collected articles in A. Berg et al. (eds), *Harald Hardråde* (Oslo: Dreyers Forlag, 1966), but only if one can read Norwegian.

On the king of Norway's campaign and the battles of Fulford Gate and Stamford Bridge, see Kelly DeVries, *The Norwegian Invasion of England in 1066* (Woodbridge: The Boydell Press, 1999). Charles Jones, *The Forgotten Battle of 1066: Fulford* (Stroud: The History Press, 2009) claims to have located the battlefield of Fulford Gate, but there is reason to have doubt.

On the immediate aftermath of the Battle of Hastings through the end of William's reign the best studies are Ann Williams, *The English and the Norman Conquest* (Woodbridge: The Boydell Press, 1995) and Hugh M. Thomas, *The Norman Conquest: England After William the Conqueror* (Lanham: Rowman and Littlefield Publishers, 2008).

Translations of the most commonly-used sources on the battle can be found in Stephen Morillo (ed.), *The Battle of Hastings: Sources and Interpretations* (Woodbridge: The Boydell Press, 1996), but many of these are quite dated and have been supplanted by more recent editions and translations from the Oxford University Press' Medieval Texts in Translation series: William of Poitiers, *The Gesta Guillelmi of William of Poitiers*, ed. and trans. R.H.C. Davis and M. Chibnall (1998); Guy of Amiens, *Carmen de hastingae proelio*, ed. C. Morton and A. Muntz (1972); William of Jumièges, *The Gesta Normanorum ducum of William of Jumièges, Orderic Vitalis, and Robert of Torigni*, ed. and trans. E.M.C. van Houts, 2 vols. (1995); John of Worcester, *The Chronicle of John of Worcester*, ed. R.R. Darlington and P. McGurk, trans. J. Bray and P. McGurk, 2 vols. (1995); Henry of Huntingdon, *Historia Anglorum: The History of the English People*, ed. and trans. D. Greenway (1996); William of Malmesbury, *Gesta regum Anglorum: The History of the English Kings*, ed. and trans. R.A.B. Mynors, R.M. Thomson, and M. Winterbottom, 2 vols. (1998); and Orderic Vitalis, *The Ecclesiastical History of Orderic Vitalis*, ed. and trans. M. Chibnall, 6 vols. (1969–80). The best edition and translation of *The Anglo-Saxon Chronicle* remains Charles Plummer and John Earle (eds), *Two of the Saxon Chronicles Parallel*, 2 vols. (Oxford: 1892), although the translations by G.N. Garmonsway (London: J.M. Dent and Sons Ltd, 1953) and M.J. Swanton (New York: Routledge, 1998) are solid. The best presentation of the Bayeux Tapestry is Stenton's mentioned above. The three best sagas containing Harald Hardrada's life are all now in English translation: Snorri Sturluson, *King Harald's Saga: Harald Hardradi of Norway*, trans. Magnus Magnusson and Hermann Pálsson (Harmondsworth: Penguin Books, 1966; *Morkinskinna: The Earliest Icelandic Chronicle of the Norwegian Kings (1030-1157)*, trans. Theodore M. Andersson and Kari Ellen Gade (Ithaca: Cornell University Press, 2000); and *Fagrskinna, a Catalogue of the Kings of Norway*, trans. Alison Finlay (Leiden: Brill, 2004).

Finally, Marjorie Chibnall's *The Debate on the Norman Conquest* (Manchester: Manchester University Press, 1999) contains the history of the history of the Norman Conquest. She offers little interpretation of the battle itself, but her accounts of how the Conquest has been presented by historians since the Middle Ages are fascinating.

INDEX

Entries of specific focus in **bold**.

Adela, countess of Blois, daughter of William 49

Adelaide of Normandy 24

Aelred of Rielvaux 16

Agincourt (battle) 172

Akeman Street 181, 197

Alexander II, pope 33, 41, 179

Alfred the Great, king of England 5, 8, 174, 176, 178, 182

Alfred Aetheling 7, 9

Alresford 178

Alton 178

Anglo-Saxon Chronicle 61, 63, 66, 68, 115, 126, 181

armour 36–7, 39, 70–2, 74, 76, 90, **130–4**, 136–49

arms 36–7, 39, 70–2, 74, 76, 90, **130–4**, 136–49

Arnulf, count of Flanders 78

Arthur, duke of Brittany 42

Athelred, king of England 7–8, 30, 169

Athelstan, king of England 6–7

Augustine, Saint 188

Aylesbury 181

Bagshot 178

Baldwin I, count of Flanders 78

Baldwin V, count of Flanders 12, 17, 28–30, 35, 59, 78

Baldwin IX, count of Flanders 80

Barking Abbey 202

Basingstoke 178

Bath 170

Battle (town, abbey, and site) 3–4, 10, **124–30**, 135–6, **150–67**, 183

Bayeux 26, 35, **47–50**, 125

Bayeux Tapestry 4, 12–13, 20, 26, 27–8, 31–3, 35–9, 49–51, 55–6, 65–6, 70, 73, 90, 103, 116, 125, **130–49**, 179

Beauport 116

Beowulf 9

Berkhamstead (town and castle) 180–1, **197–8**

Bertrand du Guesclin, duke of Brittany 53–4

Bexhill 103–5, 115

Bodiam (town and castle) 105, 116, 120, **183–4**

Bonneville-sur-Touques 35

Bosham Church 149
Boulogne (and Boulognese) 39, 137
Bourton on the Water 175
Brede, river 135
Brittany (and Bretons) 27, 30, 35, 42, 49, 137
Broken Tower *see* Richborough
Brunanburh (battle) 5–7, 9
Bulverhythe 105, 115

Caen (town and castle) 25–6, 30, 35, **42–7**
Caldbec Hill 136, 167
Canterbury (city and cathedral) 17, 116, 125, 173–5, 179, 184, 187, **188–93**, 201
Carisbrooke Castle 91
Carmen de Hastingae proelio 3, 26, 134, **137–49**, 169, 174, 176, 181
Ceclia, abbess, daughter of William 45–6
Charles VII, king of France 42, 49
Charles the Bold, duke of Burgundy 82
Chaucer, Geoffrey 182, 191
Chester 180
Chichester 175, 178
Cirencester 175
Claudius, Roman emperor 173
Cnut, king of England 7–8, 30, 50, 60, 70, 107, 179
Colchester Castle 58
Conan II, duke of Brittany 27, 32
Constantine, Roman emperor 98

Constantinople, 80
Copsig 61
Cripps Corner 121
Cromwell, Oliver 92, 196
Crusades 48–9

D-Day 38
Danevirke **84–5**
Denmark (and Danes) 7, 19, 60, 83–6
Derwent River 98–100
Dinan (town, castle, and siege) **53–5**
Dissolution of the Monasteries 91, 119, 156, 163, 189
Dives River 26, 35, 37–9, **56–7**
Dol (castle and siege) 27, 32, **51**
Domesday Book 177, 180
Dover (town and castle) 7, 10, 171–4, **185–7**
Dumfermline 63, 66, **91**
Dungeness 105
dysentery 171–2

Eadred, king of England 7–8
Ealdgyth, queen of England 180
Ealdred, archbishop of York 168, 179–82
Eadwig, king of England 6, 8
Edgar I, king of England 7–8, 17, 169
Edgar Atheling 7–8, 19, 168–9, 172, 180–1, 197
Edith, queen of England 7–9, 14–15, 20, 31–2, 178
Edith Swan-neck 1–2

Edmund II Ironside, king of
England 7–8, 19, 168
Edward I, king of England 34
Edward II, king of England 92, 98
Edward the Black Prince 190
Edward the Confessor, king of
England 8–11, 14, 16–21, 31–4,
50, 58, 70, 107, 175, 177–8
Edward the Martyr, king of
England 7–8
Edwin II, king of Northumbria 97
Edwin, earl of Mercia 16, 68–9,
168, 180–1, 197
Elizabeth I, queen of England 91
Emma, queen of England 7–9, 11,
30–1, 49
English Channel 31, 35–7, 39–40,
56, 63, 90, 101, 106–7, 124, 170,
173, 187
Enguerrand II, count of
Boulougne 24
Ermine Street 175
Eustace II, count of Boulogne 10,
28, 35, 148
Exeter 175

Fagrskinna 72, 74
Falaise (town and castle) 22, **41–2**
Farnham 178
Fécamp Abbey 35, **50–1**, 107, 116
feigned retreat 73, 141–2, 145
First World War 86
Flanders (Flemings) 10, 12, 17,
28–30, 32, 35, 59, 61, 137
Formigny (battle) 49
Fosse Way 175

Frederick the Great, king 23
French Revolution 44, 47
Fulford Gate (town and battle)
68–9, 76, **93–4**, 168–9

Geoffrey, count of Anjou 26–7
Geoffrey II Martel, count of Anjou
25
Ghent 79
Gifford 148
Godwin, earl of Wessex 7–9,
12–13, 31, 52, 61, 78, 91, 106–7,
148, 178
Gough Map 178, 181
Gruffydd ap Llywelyn, king of
Gwynedd 14
Guildford 178
Guildhall 178
Guthrum, king of the Danes 174
Guy of Amiens *see Carmen*
Guy of Ponthieu, count 25–6, 28
Gyrth Godwinson, earl of East
Anglia 10, 13, 118, 139–41, 145,
147, 168

Halletoren (Bruges) 81–2
Harald Hardrada, king of Norway
19, 39–40, 59–63, 66–77, 87–99,
114, 117, 135, 169
Harold I Harefoot, king of
England 8–9, 30, 178
Harold II Godwinson, king of
England *passim*
Harthacnut, king of England 8–9,
31, 60
Harwell 180

Hastings (battle) **134–49**, *passim*
Hastings (town and castle) 103, 105–7, 114–15, **118–20**, 121–3, 135, 137, 150, 168–9, 173, 176, 183
Hedesby **84–5**
Henry I, king of England 42, 46, 49
Henry II, king of England 42, 46, 51, 73, 92, 187, 201
Henry IV, king of England 190
Henry VIII, king of England 189
Henry I, king of France 12, 24–7
Henry III, Holy Roman Emperor 29
Henry of Huntingdon 16, 70
Hereford 16
Herleva, mother of William the Conqueror 22–3
Hog's Back 178
Holy Blood (basilica and relic) 80
Hugh of Ponthieu, count 26, 148
Humber River 67
Hundred Years War 42, 48–9, 53, 55, 58
Hythe 173

Ickfield Way 175

Jerusalem 12, 22
Joan of Arc 58
John, king of England 42, 46, 68, 92
John of Salisbury 14
John of Worcester 69, 180

Judith of Flanders, wife of Tostig 75
Julius Caesar 38, 47, 173, 185

Kingston-upon-Thames 178
Kirkdale 15

Laxdæla Saga 76
Le Crotoy, 37, 40
Leo IX, pope 28–30, 179
Leofwine Godwinson, earl of Kent 10, 14, 139–41, 145, 168
Lewes 121
Lincoln 175
Lindesfarne Abbey, 5, 64
Lodewijk van Gruuthuse 82
London 17, 53, 69, 71, 115, 118, 120–1, 135, 169, 174–6, 178, 180–1, 183, 187, 191, **200–3**
London Bridge 175–6, 200–1
Lydd 105
Lympne 173, **184**

Maidstone 120
Maine 27, 30, 52
Malcolm III, king of Scotland 63, 66, 91
Maldon (battle) 7
Malfosse 148
Maresfield 121
Mary, duchess of Burgundy 82
Matilda, queen 28–30, 42–5, 49, 181
Maximilian, Holy Roman Emperor 82
Michelangelo 82

Mont-Saint-Michel 27–8, 49, **54–6**
Monty Python and the Holy Grail 183
Morkere, earl of Northumbria 16, 68–9, 168, 180–1, 197
Morkinskinna 72
Mortemer (battle) 24, 56
Mortlake 180
Motte-and-bailey castle 52–3, 91, 97–8, 118–20, 196–7

Nicholas II, pope 30, 179
Norfolk 101
Normandy 23–57, 107, 114, 125, 169
Normans, *passim*
Normans Bay 104
Northumbria 13–17, 61, 68–9, 74
Norway (Norwegians) 7, 19, 60–3, 66–77, 90–1
Norwegian Kings Saga 58–60, 63, 66–7, 69–75, 86

Odo of Bayeux, bishop 22, 26, 47–9, 125, 134, 145, 194
Olaf, saint and king of Norway 87
Old Romney 105–6
Old St Helen's Church, Ore **121–3**
Old Winchelsea 105–6
Orderic Vitalis 33, 59–60, 118
Orkney Islands 60, 66
Orne River 25
Oslo 60–1, **87–90**
Ouse River 53, 68–9, 93, 98
Oxford 178, 181

Papal banner 41, 124
Peterborough Abbey 172
Pevensey (town and castle) 102–7, **108–14**, 115–16, 118, 120, 172–3, 176, 187
Philip II Augustus, king of France 42, 47, 51
Philip the Good, duke of Burgundy 82
Pyx Chamber, Westminster Abbey 17–18

Rameslie 107
Reading 178–80
Reculver 173
relics 127
Rhuddlan 14
Ricall 68, 91, **93**
Richard I Lionheart, king of England 46
Richard I, duke of Normandy 11, 50
Richard II, duke of Normandy 31, 42, 50
Richborough (town and castle) 171–5, **187–9**
Robert I, duke of Normandy 22–4, 42
Robert II Curthose, duke of Normandy 125
Robert, archbishop of Rouen 24
Robert of Eu, count 26, 118
Robert of Jumièges, archbishop of Canterbury 10
Robert of Mortain, count 22, 114, 197

Rochester (town and castle) 116, 120, 175, 183, **191, 194**

Roman(s) 5, 68, 91–8, 101, 103, 106–10, 112, 115–16, 120–1, 135, 170–5, 178, 181, 183–90, 201–2

Romney 103, 105–6, 170, 173

Romney Marsh 105, 170, 184

Roskilde **83–4**

Rother, river 105, 117, 183

Rouen 35, 44, 58

Rye 105, 107, 121, 173

Saint Donatian Church **78–80**

Saint-Valery-sur-Somme 37, 40, **57–8**

Sandhurst 183

Sandwich 172–3

Saxon Shore Forts 3, 101, 171–2, 174, 184–7

Scarborough 67, **91–2**

Scotland (and Scots) 63, 66, 91

Second World War 42, 47, 50, 107, 114, 119, 185

Sedlescombe 116, 121, 135

Senlac Hill 136, 167

Shakespeare, William 182

Shetland Islands 66

shield-wall 68–9, **73**, 74–7, 98, 136–7, 139, 141, 144–6, 152, 164, 166

ships 35–8, **61–6**, 68, 83, 88–9, 93, 107

Snorri Sturluson 60, 67, 70, 85

Somme River 37–8, 44, 57, 101

Southwark (town and cathedral) 176–7, 201

St Albans 181

St Augustine's Abbey 189–90

St Mary de Castro, Dover 171, 185

St Mary's Church, Westham **111**

St Mary's Parish Church, Battle **163–4**

Stamford Bridge (town and battle) 40, 67, 69–78, 87, **98–100**, 115, 117, 135, 169

Stane Street 178

Staplehurst 120

Stephen, king of England 175

Steyning 107

Stigand, archbishop of Canterbury 168, 179–80

Stone Street 184

Stour River 173

Stutfall Castle 184

Sweyn II Estridsson, king of Denmark 19, 60, 83–5

Sweyn Forkbeard, king of Denmark 7, 10, 19, 60

Sweyn Godwinson 12

Tadcaster 71

Taillefer 138

Templeborough 175

Tetsworth 181

Thames, estuary and river 17, 173, 175–8, 196, 201

Thanet, isle of 173

Thomas à Becket, archbishop of Canterbury 190, 192, 201

Tostig Godwinson, earl of Northumbria 10, 13–17, 31–2, 59–61, 63–100, 114, 117, 135, 169

Tower of London 53, **202–3**
Trondheim **86–7**
Tudors 114
Tynemouth 66

Uckfield 121
Urban II, pope 49

Val-ès-Dunes (battle) 24–5, 56
Varaville (battle) 27, 56
Vikings 5–6, 15, 48, 50, 58, 64–5,
    84–5, 88–91, 97
Vita Edwardi Regis 32

Wace 25
Wales 14, 31, 52
Wallingford (town and castle)
    177–81, **195–7**
Walter of Hereford, bishop 181
Waltham (town and abbey) 2, 149
Waltheof, earl of
    Northamptonshire and
    Huntingdonshire 168
Wantsum Channel 173, 187
Watling Street 16, 120–1, 173–5,
    178, 180–1, 184, 187, 191, 201

Weald 116, 183
Wessex 61–2
Westminster (town and abbey) 17,
    21, 169, 182, **198–200**
White Cliffs, Dover 185
Wight, Isle of 38, 61, 61–3, **90–1**,
    101, 178
William I the Conqueror, king of
    England *passim*
William II Rufus, king of England
    18, 125–6, 198
William of Jumièges 26, 181
William of Malmesbury 33, 59, 74,
    126
William of Poitiers 2–3, 11, 33, 103,
    117, 134–5, 137, **139–49**, 169–71,
    174–7, 181, 187
Winchelsea 106, 173
Winchester 121, 176–9
Witena-gemot 17–18, 33, 168
Wroxeter 16, 173, 175
Wulfstan of Worcester, bishop
    180

York 14, 52–3, 68–72, 77, 93, **94–8**,
    168, 175